Schöningh

W0379739

EinFach
Englisch
Unterrichtsmodell

Series Editor: Hans Kröger

Don DeLillo

# Falling Man


by
Michael Bähr
Kirsten Juhas

edited by
Hans Kröger

Audio-CD
Einzelarbeit
Partnerarbeit
Gruppenarbeit
Unterrichtsgespräch
Schreibauftrag
Hausaufgabe
filmische Präsentation
Projekt, offene Aufgabe
kreative Aufgabe
szenisches Spiel, Rollenspiel

# Vorwort

Der Titel der Reihe **EinFach Englisch** verdeutlicht Zielsetzung und Programm zugleich. Einerseits soll Schülerinnen und Schülern auf einfache Art und Weise der Zugang zu klassischen, aber auch neuen literarischen Werken und Filmen ermöglicht werden, andererseits sollen Lehrerinnen und Lehrern in der Praxis erprobte Unterrichtsmodelle angeboten werden, die die wichtigsten methodisch-didaktischen Ansätze ihres Faches Englisch abdecken. Dabei sind die Modelle direkt, ohne langes Einlesen einsetzbar und stellen Unterrichtsarbeit konkret vor. Als besonders hilfreich für die Praxis haben sich dabei folgende Aspekte erwiesen, die für die Gestaltung der Reihe wesentlich sind:

- Überblick über **Figurenkonstellation**, ggf. **Filmszenen** und **Inhalt**
- **Klausuren** mit **Erwartungshorizont**
- **Arbeitsblätter, Tafelbilder** und **Leitfragen** für den Unterricht
- **Piktogramme** als Hinweise auf **Unterrichts**- und **Arbeitsformen**

Das Prinzip der **„Components“** ermöglicht darüber hinaus den variablen Einsatz der Modelle in unterschiedlich konzipierten Unterrichtsreihen. Dabei stehen Machbarkeit und Praxisnähe stets im Vordergrund.

**Das vorliegende Modell bezieht sich auf folgende Textausgabe: Don DeLillo, Falling Man, hrsg. von Helga Korff, Cornelsen 2010 (ISBN 978-3-06-031260-3)**

**Sprachliche Betreuung: Anne Schülke**


Westermann Schroedel Diesterweg Schöningh Winklers GmbH
Braunschweig, Paderborn, Darmstadt

www.schoeningh-schulbuch.de
Schöningh Verlag, Jühenplatz 1–3, 33098 Paderborn



Druck 5 4 3 2 1 / Jahr 2015 14 13 12 11
Die letzte Zahl bezeichnet das Jahr dieses Druckes.

Umschlaggestaltung: Jennifer Kirchhof
Druck und Bindung: westermann druck GmbH, Braunschweig

ISBN 978-3-14-041181-3

# Getting started

What do you see in the first photo?

Describe the second photo. Comparing it to the first one, how do you feel about it?

# Falling Man

# Die Figuren

**Keith Neudecker**

Der neununddreißigjährige, groß gewachsene und blonde Keith Neudecker ist als Jurist für die Immobiliengesellschaft Royer Properties tätig, als ihn die Anschläge vom 11. September 2001 jäh aus seiner Arbeit im Büro der Firma im Nordturm des World Trade Centers reißen. Zum Zeitpunkt des Attentats lebt er bereits seit eineinhalb Jahren getrennt von seiner Frau Lianne Glenn, die er acht Jahre zuvor geheiratet hatte und mit der er den gemeinsamen siebenjährigen Sohn Justin hat. Er kehrt zwar unmittelbar nach seiner Flucht aus den Türmen ins Apartment seiner Exfrau zurück, beginnt jedoch hinter ihrem Rücken eine kurze Affäre mit einer Frau, deren Aktentasche er bei seiner Flucht mitgenommen hatte. Seine große Leidenschaft gehört dem Pokerspiel, zu dem er sich vor dem 11. September einmal wöchentlich in seinem Apartment in der Nähe des World Trade Centers mit fünf weiteren Männern getroffen hatte. Da jedoch zwei von ihnen in den Türmen umkommen und ein dritter lebensgefährlich verletzt wird, flüchtet Keith im Folgenden immer wieder an die anonymen Spieltische von Las Vegas, wo er auch einen seiner früheren Mitspieler wiedertrifft. Obwohl DeLillos Protagonist äußerlich nur geringe Blessuren davongetragen hat (Schnittwunden und eine Handgelenksverletzung), so ist er doch dauerhaft traumatisiert durch die Ereignisse des 11. Septembers, vor allem durch den Tod seines engsten Freundes und Pokerbruders Rumsey, der in den Türmen in seinen Armen gestorben ist.

**Lianne Glenn**

Die achtunddreißigjährige Lianne Glenn ist dunkelhaarig und schlank. Wie ihre Mutter Nina Bartos, zu der sie ein sehr enges Verhältnis hat, ist sie kunstinteressiert, allerdings haben ihre Studien und Reisen nach Europa und in den Nahen Osten nicht für eine Universitätskarriere, sondern nur für eine Tätigkeit als freiberufliche Lektorin gereicht. Obwohl sie ihren Vater Jack Glenn nur selten sehen konnte, da ihre Eltern sich schon früh getrennt hatten, hing Lianne sehr an ihrem Vater und leidet noch immer daran, dass er sich aus Angst vor einer beginnenden Demenzerkrankung das Leben nahm, als sie zweiundzwanzig war. Die grundsätzliche Angst, aufgrund dieser genetischen Disposition ebenfalls einen Gedächtnisverlust zu erleiden, treibt auch Lianne um. Sie engagiert sich seit zwei Jahren ehrenamtlich als Leiterin einer Alzheimer-Gruppe, die aus sieben im Anfangsstadium erkrankten Personen besteht und die einmal die Woche ihre zunehmend rarer werdenden Erinnerungen in narrativer Form festzuhalten versuchen. Weitere Möglichkeiten, ihren diversen Krankheits- und Verlustängsten, die sich durch die Anschläge vom 11. September weiter intensiviert haben, zu begegnen, bieten Lianne zum einen ausgedehnte Joggingrunden, zum anderen die Auseinandersetzung mit dem christlichen Glauben, in dem sie etwas Halt zu finden vermeint. Während ihrer Streifzüge durch New York trifft sie mehrfach auf den Falling Man, von dessen Aktionen sie fasziniert ist.

**Justin**

Der zu Beginn des Romans siebenjährige Justin ähnelt seinem Vater Keith Neudecker sowohl hinsichtlich seiner blonden Haarfarbe als auch im Hinblick auf seine Introvertiertheit. Zusammen mit seinen beiden Freunden, den Geschwistern Katie und Robert, entwickelt er ganz eigene Formen der Wahrnehmung und Verarbeitung der Geschehnisse vom 11. September. Die Kinder suchen nicht nur mit dem Fernglas den Himmel nach Flugzeugen ab, sondern sprechen nur noch in einsilbigen Wörtern, angeblich, weil ein gewisser Mann namens Bill Lawton, der mutmaßliche Herr über die Flugzeuge, das auch so macht. Außerdem bestreitet Justin vehement, dass der Einsturz des World Trade Centers bereits erfolgt sei, was seine Mutter Lianne stark verunsichert.

**Florence Givens**

Florence Givens, die Besitzerin jener Aktentasche, die Keith Neudecker zufällig bei seiner Flucht aus dem einstürzenden Nordturm in die Hände fällt, ist eine hellhäutige, vollschlanke Afro-Amerikanerin Ende dreißig, die bis zum Zeitpunkt des Unglücks für die Firma Preston Webb im World Trade Center gearbeitet hatte. Als Keith sie ausfindig macht und aufsucht, nutzt sie die Gelegenheit, ihm ihre Erlebnisse vom Tag des Attentats zu schildern, die sich teilweise mit seinen Eindrücken überschneiden. Die Möglichkeit, durch die Gespräche mit Keith und die daraus resultierende Affäre das Geschehene aufzuarbeiten, veranlasst sie zu der Aussage, er habe ihr das Leben gerettet. Dem Trauma vom 11. September geht bei ihr ein weiteres persönliches Trauma voraus: ihr Exmann, mit dem sie zehn Jahre zuvor für eine kurze Zeit verheiratet war, ist kurz nach der Trennung in volltrunkenem Zustand bei einem Autounfall ums Leben gekommen, wofür dessen Mutter ihr die Schuld gibt.

**Nina Bartos**

Die emeritierte Kunstprofessorin Nina Bartos, die an den Universitäten von Kalifornien und New York lehrte, ist bereits zu Anfang des Romans durch eine Knieoperation geschwächt, auf starke Medikamente angewiesen und verstirbt nach zweieinhalb Jahren im weiteren Handlungsverlauf der Geschichte. Ihr wissenschaftliches Spezialgebiet ist der italienische Künstler Giorgio Morandi (1890–1964), von dem sie sogar zwei wertvolle Stillleben besitzt. Diese sind ein Geschenk ihres Geliebten Martin Ridnour alias Ernst Hechinger, mit dem sie seit zwanzig Jahren liiert ist, obwohl dieser überwiegend in Europa lebt und dort verheiratet ist. Ebenso wenig wie seine familiären Verhältnisse interessiert sie seine politisch prekäre Vergangenheit. Allerdings streitet sie mehrfach mit ihm über die Hintergründe der Attentate vom 11. September, woraufhin sich die beiden zunehmend entfremden. Von dem Vater ihrer Tochter Lianne, dem Architekten Jack Glenn, lebte sie schon lange vor dessen Tod getrennt. Liannes Hochzeit mit Keith hält sie von Anfang an für einen Fehler.

**Jack Glenn**

Aus den wenigen Informationen, die der Roman zu Liannes Vater Jack Glenn bietet, geht hervor, dass er Architekt war und bei einem Projekt auf einer griechischen Insel Nina Bartos kennenlernte. Ihre Beziehung, aus der nur die eine Tochter hervorgeht, scheitert schon bald. Als der aktive, motorsport- und jagdbegeisterte Mann von seiner Demenzerkrankung erfährt, nimmt er sich kurz entschlossen mit einem Gewehr das Leben, nicht ohne seine Tochter noch einmal anzurufen und sie über seinen Zustand zu informieren. Dieses letzte Telefongespräch beschäftigt Lianne bis in die unmittelbare Erzählgegenwart hinein.

**Martin Ridnour/ Ernst Hechinger**

Der vielreisende und vielbeschäftigte Kunsthändler und -sammler Martin Ridnour ist eine dubiose Figur. Seit über zwanzig Jahren ist er der Geliebte von Liannes Mutter Nina, der er sogar wertvolle Gemälde und alte Passfotos für ihr Apartment schenkt. Sein Akzent und sein Äußeres verraten seine deutsche Herkunft. Nina weiß zwar, dass er in Europa verheiratet ist und eigentlich Ernst Hechinger heißt, gibt aber ihrer Tochter nur widerwillig Auskunft darüber, dass ihr Geliebter in den Sechzigerjahren Mitglied der Kommune I war, sich zur Zeit der Roten Brigaden in Italien aufhielt und sogar polizeilich gesucht wurde, auch wenn er nicht auf dem bekannten Fahndungsplakat der RAF abgebildet ist, das er wie einen Schatz hütet. Bezüglich der Anschläge auf das World Trade Center vertritt er die These, dass es eine Parallele gebe zwischen den Terrorzellen der RAF und den Attentätern vom 11. September.

**David Janiak (Falling Man)**

Hinter dem Aktionskünstler des Falling Man verbirgt sich der studierte Schauspieler und Dramaturg David Janiak, der im Alter von neununddreißig Jahren nicht etwa bei einem seiner zahlreichen riskanten Sprünge von Gebäuden wie der Carnegie Hall, Kirchtürmen und Brücken, sondern eines natürlichen Todes stirbt. Lianne begegnet ihm zweimal während ihrer Streifzüge durch New York und ist beeindruckt von dem Mut und der Entschlossenheit des Kunstaktivisten, der wegen seiner Aktionen, obwohl er einen Auffanggurt trägt, im ungebremsten Fall dennoch jedes Mal Leib und Leben sowie in einigen Fällen die Verhaftung durch die Polizei und Schläge von Passanten riskiert. Seine Intention besteht darin, immer wieder an diejenigen Menschen zu erinnern, die als *jumpers* bezeichnet werden, da sie am 11. September aus den brennenden Türmen des World Trade Centers in den Tod gesprungen sind.

**The Siblings**

Die „Siblings" werden von Lianne so genannt, da sie sich die tatsächlichen Namen der fantasiebegabten Katie und ihres jüngeren und als schüchtern bezeichneten Bruders Robert nicht merken kann. Die beiden Geschwister und ihre Mutter Isabel leben zehn Blocks von der Wohnung ihres besten Freundes Justin entfernt, mit dem sie gemeinsam ihre eigene Theorie hinsichtlich der Katastrophe vom 11. September entwickeln und einen Mythos um einen geheimnisvollen Mann, der Robert zufolge Bill Lawton heißt, konstruieren. Katie behauptet zudem, vom Fenster ihrer Wohnung aus den Einschlag des ersten Flugzeugs beobachtet zu haben.

**The Alzheimer group** Die Alzheimer-Gruppe, die seit circa 1999 ehrenamtlich von Lianne geleitet wird, besteht aus sieben Mitgliedern, die sich einmal die Woche treffen, um aus therapeutischen Gründen Erinnerungen schriftlich festzuhalten. Die Ergebnisse des Schreibprozesses werden laut vor der Gruppe vorgetragen und mit dem jeweiligen Vornamen und dem Anfangsbuchstaben des Nachnamens signiert: Rosellen S., Benny T., Omar H., Carmen G., Benny T., Anna C., und Curtis B., letzterer mit einundachtzig Jahren der Älteste. Da Lianne ihrerseits einen für sie heilsamen Nutzen aus der Erinnerungsarbeit ihrer Schützlinge zieht, möchte sie nach dem 11. September die Frequenz der Veranstaltung auf zweimal pro Woche erhöhen, muss aber bald einsehen, dass das nicht im Sinne der Teilnehmer ist und dass die Mitglieder, allen voran Rosellen S., zunehmend ihr Orientierungs- und Erinnerungsvermögen einbüßen und nicht mehr in der Lage sind, an den Treffen teilzunehmen.

**The poker players** Keiths Pokerrunde, die für ihn den Höhepunkt der Woche bedeutete und seit der Trennung von Lianne und Justin eineinhalb Jahre zuvor zu seinem Lebensinhalt geworden war, bestand vor dem Attentat vom 11. September aus sechs Mitspielern. Drei von ihnen wurden nur beim Nachnamen genannt (Dockery, Rumsey, Hovanis), zwei beim Vornamen (Demetrius und Keith), und einer beim vollen Namen (Terry Cheng). Da Rumsey und Hovanis in den Türmen ihr Leben verlieren und Demetrius schwerste Verbrennungen erleidet, finden die wöchentlichen Treffen, die jeden Mittwochabend in Keiths Apartment stattgefunden haben, mit dem Attentat auf das World Trade Center ein abruptes Ende.

**Hammad** Der junge Araber Hammad, dessen genaues Alter und Herkunftsland der Leser nicht erfährt, studiert Architektur und/oder Ingenieurwissenschaften in Hamburg, wo er seit zehn Jahren in der Marienstraße zusammen mit weiteren zukünftigen Attentätern lebt. Der kräftige, aber ungeschickte junge Mann ist zu Beginn noch hin- und hergerissen zwischen seiner Sehnsucht nach einem ‚normalen' Leben, das er in Ansätzen mit seiner syrisch-türkischen Freundin Leyla erlebt, und der strengen religiösen Askese der Bruderschaft, die der Anführer der Hamburger Terrorzelle, Amir (Mohamed Atta), ihm vorlebt. Hammad verkörpert den Typus des Mitläufers, der nur durch das Charisma von Amir und durch seinen Aufenthalt in einem Trainingscamp in Afghanistan, von dem in kurzen Rückblenden berichtet wird, die Bereitschaft entwickelt, den Märtyrertod am 11. September zu sterben. Da er sich als Schüler einer amerikanischen Flugschule als nicht talentiert genug erweist, selbst ein Flugzeug zu steuern, ist es seine Aufgabe, Wache zu schieben an Bord derjenigen Maschine, die entführt wird, um in den Nordturm des World Trade Centers einzuschlagen.

# Der Inhalt

Der Roman behandelt die Traumatisierung einer gesamten Nation durch die Terroranschläge auf das World Trade Center vom 11. September 2001 am Beispiel der in New York lebenden Familie Neudecker, lässt gleichzeitig jedoch auch keinen Zweifel an den bereits vor diesem Datum existierenden zerrütteten Familienverhältnissen, Ängsten und Obsessionen seiner Protagonisten, für die es nach der Katastrophe noch weniger Halt gibt als zuvor.
Keith Neudecker, ein neununddreißigjähriger Mitarbeiter einer Anwaltskanzlei, entkommt nur knapp und scheinbar lediglich von äußerlichen Blessuren gezeichnet dem durch den Aufprall des Flugzeugs vom Einsturz bedrohten Nordturm des World Trade Centers. Blutverschmiert und mit einer fremden Aktentasche in der Hand sucht er mechanisch Zuflucht bei seiner von ihm nach achtjähriger Ehe getrennt lebenden achtunddreißigjährigen Frau Lianne, die als freiberufliche Verlegerin arbeitet und mit dem gemeinsamen siebenjährigen Sohn Justin zusammenlebt. Nach einer kurzen Affäre mit der ebenfalls nur knapp dem Tode entronnenen Florence Givens, der Eigentümerin der von Keith gefundenen Aktentasche, driftet er mehr und mehr in sein altes Hobby, das Pokerspiel, ab und verbringt schließlich die meiste Zeit des Jahres als Profispieler in den Casinos von Las Vegas.
Lianne, ihrerseits traumatisiert durch den Selbstmord ihres Vaters sechzehn Jahre zuvor, leitet eine Selbsthilfegruppe für Alzheimerkranke, um ihrer Angst, ebenso wie ihr Vater an unheilbarem Gedächtnisverlust zu erkranken, zu begegnen, und beschäftigt sich zunehmend mit Glaubensfragen. Außerdem pflegt sie ihre gebrechliche Mutter Nina – eine ehemalige Kunstprofessorin, die seit zwanzig Jahren ein Verhältnis mit dem mysteriösen, seinerseits verheirateten Kunstsammler Martin Ridnour hat – bis zu deren Tod und trifft auf ihren Streifzügen durch New York immer wieder auf den Kunstaktivisten David Janiak, der mit spektakulären Sprüngen von Brücken und anderen Objekten die Erinnerung an die Opfer der Terroranschläge gegenwärtig zu halten beabsichtigt.
Der komplexe, durch Perspektivwechsel, Zeitsprünge und Rückblenden regelrecht ‚zersplitterte' Text gliedert sich strukturell gesehen in drei Teile auf, die unterschiedlichen Zeiträumen zuzuordnen sind: der erste Teil („Bill Lawton") spielt vom Tag der Anschläge bis zu 15 Tage danach; der zweite Teil („Ernst Hechinger") handelt überwiegend von der folgenden Zeit, bis zu 36 Tage nach den Anschlägen, während der letzte Teil („David Janiak") im Jahr 2004, also drei Jahre nach dem 11. September 2001, angesiedelt ist.
Eine Ausnahme stellen die drei Kapitel am Ende der jeweiligen Teile dar („On Marienstraße", „In Nokomis", „In the Hudson Corridor"), in denen es um den fiktiven Terroristen Hammad geht, dessen Entwicklung vom Hamburger Studenten bis hin zum Attentäter an Bord eines der Flugzeuge geschildert wird. Die Geschichte von Hammad lässt sich gewissermaßen losgelöst vom sonstigen Handlungsgeschehen lesen, bildet aber zugleich eine Art Rahmenhandlung, in der der Autor versucht, die Psyche, Lebensumstände und Motive eines militant radikalisierten Islamisten zu ergründen.
Als weitere Besonderheiten des Textes sind zum einen seine zyklische Struktur zu nennen, die sich aus dem Zusammenhang des ersten und letzten Kapitels ergibt (das letzte Kapitel geht dem ersten chronologisch unmittelbar voraus), zum anderen der die Wucht und Unmittelbarkeit der Attentate imitierende Übergang innerhalb des letzten Kapitels, in dem sich nicht nur die Perspektiven von Attentäter und Opfer überschneiden, sondern auch die wahre Ursache für Keiths schwere psychische Traumatisierung in den einstürzenden Türmen des World Trade Centers für die Leser erfahrbar wird.
In einem Interview mit dem *Zeit Magazin* vom 11. Oktober 2007 hat DeLillo sich dazu geäußert, wie er beim Verfassen des Romans vorgegangen ist:
„Bei *Falling Man* habe ich [...] die einzelnen Teile neu zusammengefügt, um eine innere Struktur zu schaffen, eine Balance, einen Rhythmus, damit bestimmte Elemente in einem

sinnvollen Abstand immer wieder auftauchen können." (http://www.zeit.de/2007/42/Don-DeLillo-Interview [26.07.11])
Diesen Ausführungen des Autors entsprechend, besteht der Roman aus einer schier unübersichtlichen Anzahl von ‚Handlungssplittern', die sich lediglich punktuell zeitlich konkret zuordnen lassen. Die folgende Strukturübersicht versucht eine grobe Orientierung zu liefern, wobei sie **ausschließlich diejenigen Zeitangaben aufführt, die eindeutig zu bestimmen sind**.

**Part One: Bill Lawton**

| chapter | plot fragments | time |
|---|---|---|
| 1 | Keith escapes from the area of destruction | 11 Sept 2001 |
| 2 | • Lianne looks back on the happy times of her marriage eight years ago (flashback)<br>• Lianne talks with her mother Nina about Keith's unexpected return | 14 Sept 2001 (3 days after 9/11)<br>17 Sept 2001 (Monday after the attacks) |
| 3 | • Keith is treated in a hospital<br>• Lianne meets Isabel, mother of the Siblings<br>• Lianne and Keith observe each other in her bedroom<br>• Keith gets an MRI in the hospital<br>• Lianne sees a photo of one of the terrorists in the newspaper<br>• Lianne talks to Carol Shoup, her boss<br>• Lianne asks Keith why he has returned to her<br>• Keith has outpatient surgery on his wrist<br>• Lianne ponders on her life while walking down Third Avenue<br>• Keith returns to his apartment near Ground Zero, where he thinks about his former poker rounds | 11 Sept 2001<br>11 Sept 2001<br>11 Sept 2001 |
| 4 | • Lianne's Alzheimer group<br>• Keith checks his mail at Lianne's apartment<br>• Lianne sees Falling Man for the first time at Grand Central Station<br>• Lianne reflects on her feelings for Keith<br>• Keith has a closer look at the briefcase he took from the WTC<br>• Isabel tells Lianne about 'Bill Lawton'<br>• Keith is disturbed in his sleep by music<br>• Lianne tries to get information from Justin<br>• Keith does rehab exercises for his wrist<br>• Lianne thinks about her father's suicide sixteen years ago (flashback)<br>• Lianne witnesses a controversial discussion between Nina and her mother's lover, Martin, about 9/11 | 21 Sept 2001 (ten days after the attacks)<br>17 Sept 2001 (Monday after the attacks) |
| 5 | • Keith visits Florence for the first time<br>• Lianne thinks that Keith has changed<br>• Lianne talks to Dr Apter<br>• the Alzheimer patients write about 9/11<br>• Keith contemplates on his new family life<br>• Lianne is annoyed by the loud music which comes from her neighbour Elena's apartment<br>• Lianne and Keith talk about Bill Lawton | 26 Sept 2001 (15 days after the attacks) |
| On Marienstr. | Hammad, Amir, and other Islamists in Hamburg | c. 1999 |

## Part Two: Ernst Hechinger

| chapter | plot fragments | time |
|---|---|---|
| 6 | • Keith arrives at Lianne's apartment<br>• Keith starts having an affair with Florence<br>• another meeting of the Alzheimer group whose members are slowly deteriorating<br>• Keith kicks against the door of the apartment from which the loud music comes<br>• Keith's poker nights (flashback)<br>• Keith, Lianne and Justin at dinner<br>• Keith walks through Central Park<br>• Lianne thinks about Keith's estrangement before their separation one and a half years ago (flashback)<br>• Lianne and Keith sit in a taxi, she reflects on their relationship<br>• Keith continues his rehab exercises<br>• Florence tells Keith that he saved her life | 11 Sept 2001 |
| 7 | • Nina and Martin continue their argument about 9/11<br>• Keith, Justin and Lianne watch poker on TV<br>• Lianne hits her neighbour, Elena<br>• Keith thinks of his best friend, Rumsey (flashback)<br>• Lianne informs Keith about her fight with Elena<br>• Lianne tells the Alzheimer patients about Keith's return to her apartment on 9/11<br>• Keith becomes more and more like his father<br>• Keith recalls Terry Cheng's skills as a poker player (flashback)<br>• Lianne thinks about her father again (flashback)<br>• Keith and Lianne watch TV, she tells him about her father's suicide<br>• Keith helps Florence to buy a new mattress<br>• Lianne repeatedly watches a video tape of the terrorist attacks | 17 Sept 2001 (Monday after the attacks) |
| 8 | • Keith contemplates on his affair with Florence<br>• Lianne meets Carol Shoup<br>• the Alzheimer patients write about the absent member, Rosellen S.<br>• Keith goes to a gym<br>• Lianne questions her mother about Martin's past<br>• Keith thinks about his former poker friends again (flashback)<br>• Lianne encounters Elena in the basement<br>• Lianne badgers Katie about Bill Lawton | 17 Sept 2001 (Monday after the attacks) |
| 9 | *parallel lines of action:*<br>• Lianne walks through the streets of NYC<br>• Keith picks up Justin from school and decides to surprise Lianne by coming to meet her<br>• Lianne's second encounter with Falling Man in the vicinity of a school<br>• Keith considers telling Lianne about Florence<br>• Lianne is waiting for Falling Man to jump<br>• Keith and Justin are looking for Lianne<br>• Falling Man jumps and stops close to Lianne | 17 Oct 2001 (36 days after the attacks) |
| In Nokomis | Hammad, Amir and other Islamists attend a flight school in Florida | summer 2001 |

**Part Three: David Janiak**

| chapter | plot fragments | time |
|---|---|---|
| 10 | • Lianne and Justin participate in a peace demonstration on Charlie Parker's birthday<br><br>• Lianne undergoes various neurological tests<br>• Keith takes part in a poker tournament in Las Vegas<br>• Lianne misses Nina who died four months earlier, she recalls her mother's funeral where she talked to Martin for the last time (flashback) | 29 Aug 2004 (three years after 9/11) |
| 11 | • Keith spends most of his time in the casinos of Las Vegas where he meets Terry Cheng<br>• Keith and Lianne have an argument about a pen<br>• Terry Cheng talks to Keith about Rumsey<br>• Keith gives Lianne a phone call when he hears about terrorists taking hostages in Russia<br>• Lianne informs Keith that she has normal morphology<br>• further phone calls between Keith and Lianne | 1/2/3 Sept 2004 |
| 12 | • Lianne goes to a Morandi exhibition in Chelsea<br>• Keith reflects on his present way of life in Las Vegas<br>• Keith and Lianne's family life<br>• Lianne tries to talk to Keith about his aggressions and their future | |
| 13 | • Lianne is summoned for jury service<br>• Lianne remembers her father (flashback)<br>• Lianne comes across David Janiak's obituary and starts looking for information on the Internet | |
| 14 | • Keith's addiction to poker<br>• Lianne goes to church and ponders on the existence of God<br>• Keith continues his rehab exercises<br>• Lianne feels the same way she did before 9/11 | |
| In the Hudson Corridor | Hammad on board the plane which is about to crash into the north tower/Keith's traumatic flight from the WTC | 11 Sept 2001 |

# The Author

The American novelist, playwright, and essayist Don DeLillo was born on November 20, 1936 in a working-class, Italian-American, North Bronx neighbourhood of New York City. In 1958, he graduated from Fordham University with a bachelor's degree in Communication Arts. Subsequently, he took a job as a copywriter at the advertising agency Ogilvy & Mather on Fifth Avenue. After leaving the agency in 1964, he started working as a freelance writer and began to work on his first novel, *Americana*, which was published in 1971. In 1979, a Guggenheim Fellowship allowed him to spend two years in Greece.

Until the present day, DeLillo has published fifteen novels, four plays, one screenplay as well as numerous short stories and essays. With each of his novels, his literary reputation in the United States and abroad increased. His eighth novel, *White Noise*, published in 1985, is considered his major breakthrough and won the National Book Award. Among DeLillo's other critically acclaimed and award-winning novels are *Libra* (1988), *Mao II* (1991), *Underworld* (1997), *Cosmopolis* (2003), *Falling Man* (2007), and, most recently, *Point Omega* (2010). He is widely regarded as one of the most important representatives of literary postmodernism, exploring themes deeply rooted in the late twentieth and early twenty-first century such as the mass media, consumerism, terrorism, conspiracy theories, the role of art and language, and the disruption of personal and national identity. Standing in the first rank with authors like Thomas Pynchon, Paul Auster, Philip Roth and Cormack McCarthy, he has become one of the most significant contemporary American novelists.

Don DeLillo has been married to Barbara Bennett since 1975 and currently lives near New York City.

# Vorüberlegungen zum Einsatz des Romans im Unterricht

Don DeLillos Roman *Falling Man* im Unterricht zu behandeln, zumal in einem Grundkurs, wie es die Vorgaben für das Zentralabitur in Nordrhein-Westfalen vorschreiben, stellt in fachwissenschaftlicher wie didaktischer Hinsicht eine große Herausforderung dar.
In Anbetracht des sprachlich-literarisch hohen Niveaus und der Komplexität des Romans, die durch DeLillos spezifisch postmodernes Erzählverfahren (Multiperspektivik, permanente Zeitsprünge, Aufsplitterung des *plots* in Fragmente) bedingt ist, ist von einer Vorablektüre kategorisch abzuraten, um einer vermutlich raschen Entmutigung auf Seiten der Schülerinnen und Schüler von vornherein entgegenzuwirken. Die Aufgabe der Lehrerin/des Lehrers besteht deshalb wie vielleicht bei kaum einem anderen der im Rahmen der Qualifikationsphase zu behandelnden Texte und Themen auch und gerade darin, bereits im Vorfeld wie auch im Verlauf der gesamten Reihe immer wieder für Entlastung zu sorgen.
Vor allem zu Beginn der Reihe erscheint ein betont kleinschrittiges, textzentriertes Vorgehen im Sinne eines *close reading* kurzer Passagen ratsam. Aufgrund der Widerstände, die *Falling Man* selbst erfahrenen Leserinnen und Lesern entgegensetzt, sind die Schülerinnen und Schüler im Verlauf der Reihe unbedingt immer wieder zum Weiterlesen zu motivieren. Auch wenn das Unterrichtsmodell, das sich weitgehend am Aufbau des Romans orientiert, thematische Schwerpunkte setzt, besteht kein Zweifel daran, dass nur eine komplette Lektüre dem Roman in seiner Vielschichtigkeit gerecht werden kann.
Erfahrungen in Zusammenhang mit der Behandlung des Romans im Unterricht haben gezeigt, dass der Text einerseits zwar mit gutem Grund als ausgesprochen schwierig eingestuft wird, andererseits aber auch eine Reihe interessanter und nach wie vor hochaktueller Themen (z. B. Terrorismus, Fundamentalismus, Spielsucht, Erinnerungskultur, zerrüttete Familienstrukturen) behandelt, die sich anschaulich und schülergerecht didaktisch aufbereiten lassen.
Don DeLillos *Falling Man* bietet darüber hinaus Anknüpfungspunkte zu anderen Aspekten des Lehrplans Englisch (SII) in Nordrhein-Westfalen, etwa zu dem Themenschwerpunkt Globalisierung und dem Bereich des interkulturellen Lernens. Als Reaktion auf neue Formen islamistischen Terrors in einer globalisierten Welt lässt sich der Roman mit dem von Samuel P. Huntington diagnostizierten *clash of civilisations* in Verbindung bringen, wobei DeLillo grundlegende gesellschaftlich-moralische Fragen aufwirft, ohne seine Leserinnen und Leser mit allzu einfachen Antworten abzuspeisen.
Diesem Unterrichtsmodell liegt die Textausgabe von Cornelsen 2010 (ISBN 978-3-06-031260-3) zugrunde, deren zahlreiche Worterklärungen und Erläuterungen die Lektüre maßgeblich erleichtern.

# Klausuren

Die beiden Klausuren, die sich auf konkrete Textstellen aus DeLillos Roman beziehen, stammen aus dem ersten Teil von *Falling Man*, da dort bereits alle Grundthemen des Textes anklingen und der Eindruck der Katastrophe noch unmittelbare Reaktionen unter den Figuren hervorruft.

In **Klausur 1** geht es um eines von zwei Streitgesprächen zwischen Nina Bartos und ihrem Geliebten Martin Ridnour/Ernst Hechinger, in dem DeLillo paradigmatisch eine amerikanische Perspektive auf eine europäische prallen lässt. Die Klausur kann zu einem relativ frühen Zeitpunkt der Romanbesprechung zum Einsatz kommen, allerdings sollten die Hauptfiguren und die Figurenkonstellation im Unterricht behandelt und die wahre Identität von Ernst Hechinger – vermutlich ein ehemaliges Mitglied der Kommune I und der Roten Brigade sowie ein Unterstützer der RAF – geklärt worden sein.

Die **zweite Klausur** beschäftigt sich mit der Bandbreite von möglichen Reaktionen auf das Unglück und der Frage nach der Rolle Gottes in Zusammenhang mit den Anschlägen, verdeutlicht am Beispiel von Liannes Alzheimer-Gruppe. Da die verschiedenen Symptome der Erkrankung in dieser Sitzung der Gruppe wenig ins Blickfeld geraten, genügt es bei dieser Klausur, im Rahmen der Charakterisierung von Lianne bereits auf die Bedeutung ihrer ehrenamtlichen Tätigkeit für ihre persönliche Biografie hingewiesen zu haben.

Ein Ausschnitt aus Martin Amis' äußerst umstrittener Kurzgeschichte „The Last Days of Muhammad Atta" bildet den **dritten Klausurvorschlag**, der eine gründliche Besprechung der Figuren Hammad und Amir (Mohamed Atta) voraussetzt. Auch die Problematik, aus westlicher Perspektive eine Annäherung an die Denkweise und Motivation der Attentäter zu versuchen, sollte in Ansätzen im Unterricht am Beispiel von *Falling Man* thematisiert worden sein. Aus dem letztgenannten Grund gibt es für diese Klausur auch keine kreative Aufgabe zur Auswahl.

# Don DeLillo, *Falling Man* (2007), part one, chapter four, p. 48, l. 4 – p. 49, l. 21

Lianne said, "Who wants to eat?"

Nina wanted to smoke. The bamboo end table stood next to the armchair now and held an ashtray, a lighter and a pack of cigarettes.

Her mother lit up. She watched, Lianne did, feeling something familiar and a little painful, how Nina at a certain point began to consider her invisible. The memory was located there, in the way she snapped shut the lighter and put it down, in the hand gesture and the drifting smoke.

"Dead wars, holy wars. God could appear in the sky tomorrow."

"Whose God would it be?" Martin said.

"God used to be an urban Jew. He's back in the desert now."

Lianne's studies were meant to take her into deeper scholarship, into serious work in languages or art history. She'd traveled through Europe and much of the Middle East but it was tourism in the end, with shallow friends, not determined inquiry into beliefs, institutions, languages, art, or so said Nina Bartos.

"It's sheer panic. They attack out of panic."

"This much, yes, it may be true. Because they think the world is a disease. This world, this society, ours. A disease that's spreading," he said.

"There are no goals they can hope to achieve. They're not liberating a people or casting out a dictator. Kill the innocent, only that."

"They strike a blow to this country's dominance. They achieve this, to show how a great power can be vulnerable. A power that interferes, that occupies."

He spoke softly, looking into the carpet.

"One side has the capital, the labor, the technology, the armies, the agencies, the cities, the laws, the police and the prisons. The other side has a few men willing to die."

"God is great," she said.

"Forget God. These are matters of history. This is politics and economics. All the things that shape lives, millions of people, dispossessed, their lives, their consciousness."

"It's not the history of Western interference that pulls down these societies. It's their own history, their mentality. They live in a closed world, of choice, of necessity. They haven't advanced because they haven't wanted to or tried to."

"They use the language of religion, okay, but this is not what drives them."

"Panic, this is what drives them."

Her mother's anger submerged her own. She deferred to it. She saw the hard tight fury in Nina's face and felt, herself, only a sadness, hearing these two people, joined in spirit, take strongly opposing positions.

Then Martin eased off, voice going soft again.

"All right, yes, it may be true."

"Blame us. Blame us for their failures."

"All right, yes. But this is not an attack on one country, one or two cities. All of us, we are targets now."

They were still talking ten minutes later when Lianne left the room. *(470 words)*

**urban** one who lives in a town or city

**shallow** not capable of thinking seriously

**sheer** nothing more than

**interfere** to take part in something, esp. without having the right to do so

**submerge** drown

**defer** (here) to submit in opinion or judgment to

**ease off** (here) relax

## Assignments

1. Summarize what Nina and Martin are talking about in the excerpt from the fourth chapter of the first part of Don DeLillo's novel *Falling Man*. (*Comprehension*)

2. Analyse Nina's and Martin's lines of argumentation concerning the reasons for the 9/11 terrorist attacks on the World Trade Center by taking their relationship and their different backgrounds into consideration. (*Analysis*)

Choose **one** of the following assignments:

**3.1** Explain and comment on the following statement by Martin from the second dispute with Nina on terrorism (part two, chapter seven, p. 114, ll. 6–9):

"Weren't the towers built as fantasies of wealth and power that would one day become fantasies of destruction? You build a thing like that so you can see it come down. The provocation is obvious." (*Comment*)

**3.2** Imagine you were invited to participate in a student panel discussion in New York City on the reasons for 9/11 and the impact of the attacks on America as a world power. Write a contribution to this discussion. (*Re-creation of text*)

# Erwartungshorizont zu Klausur 1

## Aufgabe 1 (Comprehension) – Anforderungen: The student …

| | | points | |
|---|---|---|---|
| 1 | writes an introduction which comprises central aspects: author's name, title and genre of the text from which the excerpt is taken, date of publication | 2 | |
| 2 | describes the situation and briefly outlines the constellation of the characters in the excerpt | 2 | |
| 3 | points out the topic of the argument between Nina and Martin: reasons/ motivations for the recent terrorist attacks on the World Trade Center | 2 | |
| 4 | briefly outlines Nina's position and her arguments | 5 | |
| 5 | briefly outlines Martin's position and his arguments | 5 | |
| 6 | fulfils another criterion which is related to the task (aufgabenbezogenes Kriterium) | (2) | |
| | total | 16 | |

## Aufgabe 2 (Analysis) – Anforderungen: The student …

| | | points | |
|---|---|---|---|
| 1 | examines Nina's position and her arguments/line of argumentation:<br>• religious perspective<br>• panic as driving force<br>• no 'higher' political motivation, only goal: kill as many innocent people as possible<br>• terrorists live in a closed world which has not developed into a humane society yet<br>• problem of cultural background and mentality<br>• she does not want to put any blame on America | 7 | |
| 2 | examines Martin's position and his arguments/line of argumentation:<br>• no religious motivation for the attacks, although religious language is used<br>• Western society considered as an infectious "disease" (ll. 16, 17) which has to be cured/erased<br>• terrorist attacks as a strike against America's power and leading role in world politics<br>• global inequality between rich Western and poor Eastern/Arabian societies<br>• far-reaching political, historical and economic reasons for the attacks<br>• since 9/11 everybody has become a potential target of future terrorist attacks | 7 | |
| 3 | explains and analyses Nina's personal background with regard to its apparent influence on her present position: life in the US, academic studies and profession, moderate American perspective | 4 | |
| 4 | explains and analyses Martin's personal background with regard to its influence on his present position: stay in Germany and Italy during the time of the RAF and the Red Brigades, former member of a radical left-wing organization fighting against a supposed fascist state, radical 'European' perspective | 6 | |
| 5 | fulfils another criterion which is related to the task (aufgabenbezogenes Kriterium) | (4) | |
| | total | 24 | |

## Aufgabe 3.1 (Comment) – Anforderungen: The student …

| | | points | |
|---|---|---|---|
| 1 | explains Martin's statement in her/his own words | 4 | |
| 2 | develops plausible arguments (pros and cons) to support/refute Martin's statement | 10 | |
| 3 | comes to a comprehensible conclusion | 6 | |
| 4 | fulfils another criterion which is related to the task (aufgabenbezogenes Kriterium) | (4) | |
| | total | 20 | |

## Aufgabe 3.2 (Re-creation of text) – Anforderungen: The student …

| | | points | |
|---|---|---|---|
| 1 | adopts the role of a German student participating in the panel discussion and starts his contribution in an adequate way, e. g.:<br>● briefly introduces himself/herself<br>● refers to the different national contexts (Germany/USA) | 4 | |
| 2 | explores possible reasons for the attacks, e. g.:<br>● to weaken America's leading role as a world power (economic and military dominance)<br>● prejudices against 'American way of life' as representative of Western thought and lifestyle<br>● hate/fear concerning differences in religion, morals, rights of women, etc. | 8 | |
| 3 | explores the impact of the attacks on America as a world power, e. g.:<br>● American claim of leadership symbolically destroyed<br>● first time that America has been attacked in its history<br>● concept of tolerance endangered<br>● war against terror | 8 | |
| 4 | fulfils another criterion which is related to the task (aufgabenbezogenes Kriterium) | (4) | |
| | total | 20 | |

## Kommunikative Textgestaltung – Anforderungen: Der Prüfling …

| | | points | |
|---|---|---|---|
| 1 | erstellt einen kohärenten und flüssig lesbaren Text | 5 | |
| 2 | beachtet die Normen der jeweils geforderten Textsorte | 5 | |
| 3 | belegt seine Aussagen durch konkrete Verweise und Zitate | 5 | |
| 4 | strukturiert seinen Text in erkennbare und thematisch kohärente Abschnitte | 5 | |
| 5 | stellt die Gedanken in logischer, folgerichtiger Weise dar und verknüpft diese sinnvoll | 5 | |
| 6 | gestaltet den Text ökonomisch (Vermeidung unnötiger Wiederholungen und Umständlichkeiten) | 5 | |
| | total | 30 | |

**Ausdrucksvermögen/Verfügbarkeit sprachlicher Mittel – Anforderungen: Der Prüfling ...**

| | | points | |
|---|---|---|---|
| 1 | formuliert verständlich, präzise und klar | 4 | |
| 2 | bedient sich eines sachlich wie stilistisch angemessenen und differenzierten allgemeinen Wortschatzes | 4 | |
| 3 | bedient sich eines treffenden und differenzierten thematischen Wortschatzes | 4 | |
| 4 | bedient sich in sachlich wie stilistisch angemessener Weise der fachmethodischen Terminologie | 4 | |
| 5 | bildet komplexe Satzgefüge und variiert den Satzbau | 10 | |
| 6 | löst sich von Formulierungen des Ausgangstextes und formuliert eigenständig | 4 | |
| | total | 30 | |

**Sprachrichtigkeit – Anforderungen: Der Prüfling ...**

| | | points | |
|---|---|---|---|
| | ist in der Lage, einen Text nach den Normen der sprachlichen Korrektheit zu verfassen | 30 | |

| | points | |
|---|---|---|
| **total** | 150 | |

# Don DeLillo, *Falling Man* (2007), part one, chapter five, p. 62, ll. 1–25 – p. 63, ll. 3–33

They wrote about the planes. They wrote about where they were when it happened. They wrote about people they knew who were in the towers, or nearby, and they wrote about God.

How could God let this happen? Where was God when this happened?

Benny T. was glad he was not a man of faith because he would lose it after this.

I am closer to God than ever, Rosellen wrote.

This is the devil. This is hell. All that fire and pain. Never mind God. This is hell.

Omar H. was afraid to go out on the street in the days after. They were looking at him, he thought.

I didn't see them holding hands. I wanted to see that, Rosellen wrote.

Carmen G. wanted to know whether everything that happens to us has to be part of God's plan.

I am closer to God than ever, am closer, will be closer, shall be closer.

Eugene A., in a rare appearance, wrote that God knows things we don't know.

Ashes and bones. That's what's left of God's plan.

But when the towers fell, Omar wrote.

I keep hearing they were holding hands when they jumped.

If God let his happen, with the planes, then did God make me cut my finger when I was slicing bread this morning? [...]

"God says something happens, then it happens."

"I don't respect God no more, after this."

"We sit and listen and God tells us or doesn't."

"I was walking down the street to get my hair cut. Somebody comes running."

"I was on the crapper. I hated myself later. People said where were you when it happened. I didn't tell them where I was."

"But you remember to tell us. That's beautiful, Benny."

They interrupted, gestured, changed the subject, talked over each other, shut their eyes in thought or puzzlement or in dismal re-experience of the event itself.

"What about the people God saved? Are they better people than the ones who died?"

"It's not ours to ask. We don't ask."

"A million babies die in Africa and we can't ask."

"I thought it was war. I thought it was war," Anna said. "I stayed inside and lit a candle. It's the Chinese, my sister said, who she never trusted with the bomb."

Lianne struggled with the idea of God. She was taught to believe that religion makes people compliant. This is the purpose of religion, to return people to a childlike state. Awe and submission, her mother said. This is why religion speaks so powerfully in laws, rituals and punishments. And it speaks beautifully as well, inspiring music and art, elevating consciousness in some, reducing it in others. People fall into trances, people literally go to the ground, people crawl great distances or march in crowds stabbing themselves and whipping themselves. And other people, the rest of us, maybe we're rocked more gently, joined to something deep in the soul. Powerful and beautiful, her mother said. We want to transcend, we want to pass beyond the limits of safe understanding, and what better way to do it than through make-believe. *(520 words)*

from: Don DeLillo. *Falling Man*. Berlin: Cornelsen, 2010 (2009), pp. 62–63. 

**crapper** slang term for toilet

**compliant** obedient, ready to yield to the wishes or desires of others

**awe** fear, terror

**stabbing** killing with a dagger

**whipping** to punish or chastise with a whip or rod

**transcend** to pass over or go beyond an obstacle or limit

**make-believe** pretending that things are different from how they are, imagining especially that things are better than they really are

## Assignments

1. Describe the session of Lianne's Alzheimer group as presented in the extract. (*Comprehension*)

2. Examine and compare the different positions of the group members concerning God's role in the terrorist attacks of 11 September 2001, and interpret Lianne's attitude towards religion. (*Analysis*)

Choose **one** of the following tasks:

**3.1** Explain and comment on Lianne's thought from the end of the novel (part three, chapter fourteen, p. 226, l. 1):

"God is the voice that says, 'I am not here.'" (*Comment*)

**3.2** "Where were you when it happened?" Omar H. asks Lianne (part two, chapter seven, p. 124, l. 5). Write down Lianne's personal memories of the day of the terrorist attacks, using the first person singular. (*Re-creation of text*)

# Erwartungshorizont zu Klausur 2

### Aufgabe 1 (Comprehension) – Anforderungen: The student …

| | | points | |
|---|---|---|---|
| 1 | writes an introduction which comprises central aspects: author's name, title and genre of the text from which the excerpt is taken, date of publication | 2 | |
| 2 | introduces Lianne's Alzheimer group and briefly outlines its function | 2 | |
| 3 | points out the central topic of the session: experiences of and reactions to the terrorist attacks of 11 September 2001 with regard to God's role | 2 | |
| 4 | briefly outlines how the group members experienced 9/11 and what they think about God against the background of the terrorist attacks | 8 | |
| 5 | outlines Lianne's sceptical attitude towards God and religion | 2 | |
| 6 | fulfils another criterion which is related to the task (aufgabenbezogenes Kriterium) | (2) | |
| | total | 16 | |

### Aufgabe 2 (Analysis) – Anforderungen: The student …

| | | points | |
|---|---|---|---|
| 1 | examines the different positions of the group members concerning God's role in the terrorist attacks of 9/11 and compares them with each other:<br>• complaint about God's absence | 2 | |
| 2 | • atheistic position, loss of faith and religious respect (Benny T.) | 4 | |
| 3 | • strengthening of faith (Rosellen) | 2 | |
| 4 | • concept of evil/the devil: attacks as a manifestation of hell on earth | 2 | |
| 5 | • concepts of God's responsibility, his plan and its failure (Carmen G., Eugene A.) | 4 | |
| 6 | • moral perspective: survivors better people than the ones who died? | 2 | |
| 7 | analyses and interprets Lianne's sceptical and ambivalent attitude towards God and religion which originates in her childhood and the way her mother brought her up | 8 | |
| 8 | fulfils another criterion which is related to the task (aufgabenbezogenes Kriterium) | (4) | |
| | total | 24 | |

### Aufgabe 3.1 (Comment) – Anforderungen: The student …

| | | points | |
|---|---|---|---|
| 1 | explains Lianne's thought in her own words | 4 | |
| 2 | comments on this thought by developing plausible arguments (pros and cons) and examples | 10 | |
| 3 | comes to a comprehensible conclusion | 6 | |

| | | | |
|---|---|---|---|
| 4 | fulfils another criterion which is related to the task (aufgabenbezogenes Kriterium) | (4) | |
| | total | 20 | |

### Aufgabe 3.2 (Re-creation of text) – Anforderungen: The student …

| | | points | |
|---|---|---|---|
| 1 | writes from Lianne's point of view how she experienced the day of the terrorist attacks:<br>● at home in her flat<br>● her surprise at Keith's unexpected arrival | 4 | |
| 2 | describes what Keith looked like and how she tried to wipe away the blood, dust and ash from his face and hands | 4 | |
| 3 | explains the difficult relationship of the split couple (e.g. their having been married for 8 years and having lived separately for 1½ years; Keith's obsession with poker and his male friends; his refusal to share his feelings with her) | 6 | |
| 4 | describes her ambivalent feelings caused by the terrorist attacks and Keith's arrival (e.g. shock, fear, pity, lack of communication, sudden closeness after a long period of personal distance) | 6 | |
| 5 | fulfils another criterion which is related to the task (aufgabenbezogenes Kriterium) | (4) | |
| | total | 20 | |

### Kommunikative Textgestaltung – Anforderungen: Der Prüfling …

| | | points | |
|---|---|---|---|
| 1 | erstellt einen kohärenten und flüssig lesbaren Text | 5 | |
| 2 | beachtet die Normen der jeweils geforderten Textsorte | 5 | |
| 3 | belegt seine Aussagen durch konkrete Verweise und Zitate | 5 | |
| 4 | strukturiert seinen Text in erkennbare und thematisch kohärente Abschnitte | 5 | |
| 5 | stellt die Gedanken in logischer, folgerichtiger Weise dar und verknüpft diese sinnvoll | 5 | |
| 6 | gestaltet den Text ökonomisch (Vermeidung unnötiger Wiederholungen und Umständlichkeiten) | 5 | |
| | total | 30 | |

### Ausdrucksvermögen/Verfügbarkeit sprachlicher Mittel – Anforderungen: Der Prüfling …

| | | points | |
|---|---|---|---|
| 1 | formuliert verständlich, präzise und klar | 4 | |
| 2 | bedient sich eines sachlich wie stilistisch angemessenen und differenzierten allgemeinen Wortschatzes | 4 | |
| 3 | bedient sich eines treffenden und differenzierten thematischen Wortschatzes | 4 | |

| | | | |
|---|---|---|---|
| 4 | bedient sich in sachlich wie stilistisch angemessener Weise der fachmethodischen Terminologie | 4 | |
| 5 | bildet komplexe Satzgefüge und variiert den Satzbau | 10 | |
| 6 | löst sich von Formulierungen des Ausgangstextes und formuliert eigenständig | 4 | |
| | total | 30 | |

### Sprachrichtigkeit – Anforderungen: Der Prüfling …

| | | points | |
|---|---|---|---|
| | ist in der Lage, einen Text nach den Normen der sprachlichen Korrektheit zu verfassen | 30 | |

| | points | |
|---|---|---|
| **total** | 150 | |

# Martin Amis, "The Last Days of Muhammad Atta" (2006)

Muhammad Atta wasn't like the others, because he was doing what he was doing for the core reason. The others were doing what they were doing for the core reason too, but they had achieved sublimation, by means of jihadi ardour; and their bodies had been convinced by this arrangement and had gone along with it. They ate, drank, smoked, smiled, snored; they took the stairs two at a time. Muhammad Atta's body had not gone along with it. He was doing what he was doing for the core reason and for the core reason only.

'Purify your heart and cleanse it of stains. Forget and be oblivious to the thing which is called World.' Muhammad Atta was not religious; he was not even especially political. He had allied himself with the militants because jihad was, by many magnitudes, the most charismatic idea of his generation. To unite ferocity and rectitude in a single word: nothing could compete with that. He played along with it, and did the things that impressed his peers; he collected quotations, citations, charities, pilgrimages, conspiracy theories, and so on, as other people collected autographs or beer mats. And it suited his character. If you took away all the rubbish about faith, then fundamentalism suited his character, and with an almost sinister precision.

For example, the approach to the question of women: he found the blend of aggression and alarmism highly congenial. In addition, he liked the idea of the brotherhood, although of course he exhaustively despised the current contingent, particularly his fellow pilots: Hani (the Pentagon) he barely knew, but he was continuously enraged by Marwan (the other Twin Tower) and almost fascinated by the pitch of his loathing for Ziad (the Capitol) ... Adultery punished by whipping, sodomy by burial alive: this seemed about right to Muhammad Atta. He also joined in the hatred of music. And the hatred of laughter. 'Why do you never laugh?' he was sometimes asked. Ziad would answer, 'How can you laugh when people are dying in Palestine?' Muhammad Atta never laughed, not because people were dying in Palestine, but because he found nothing funny. 'The thing which is called World.' That, too, spoke to him. World had always felt like an illusion – an unreal mockery.

'The time between you and your marriage in heaven is very short.' Ah yes, the virgins: six dozen of them – half a gross. Muhammad Atta, with his two degrees in architecture, his excellent English, his excellent German: Muhammad Atta did not believe in the virgins, did not believe in the Garden. How could he believe in such an implausibly, and dauntingly, priapic paradise? He was an apostate: that's what he was. He didn't expect paradise. What he expected was oblivion. And, strange to say, he would find neither.

He packed. He paused and stooped over the dented refrigerator, then straightened up and headed for the door. *(483 words)*

from: Martin Amis. *The Second Plane: September 11, 2001–2007*. London: Vintage, 2008, pp. 101–2.

**sublimation** transmutation into something higher, purer, or more sublime
**jihadi** relating to or advocating a jihad; see also l. 10
**ardour** warmth of emotion
**oblivious** that forgets or is given to forgetting; forgetful; see also l. 34
**jihad** a religious war of Muslims against unbelievers

**sodomy** sexual intercourse with animals

**priapic** phallic; sexual, lascivious
**apostate** one who abjures or forsakes his religious faith

**oblivion** the state or fact of forgetting or having forgotten; forgetfulness; (also) freedom from care or worry

## Assignments

1. Describe what we learn about Muhammad Atta as he is portrayed by Martin Amis on the morning of 11 September 2001. (*Comprehension*)
2. Write a characterization of Atta and examine the way one of the leaders of the terrorist attacks is presented. Consider point of view and stylistic devices. (*Analysis*)
3. Comment on Amis's portrait of Muhammad Atta and its plausibility against the background of Don DeLillo's novel *Falling Man* and of what you know about the terrorist attacks of 9/11. (*Comment*)

# Erwartungshorizont zu Klausur 3

## Aufgabe 1 (Comprehension) – Anforderungen: The student …

| | | points | |
|---|---|---|---|
| 1 | writes an introduction which comprises central aspects: the author's name, title and genre of the text from which the excerpt is taken, date of publication | 2 | |
| 2 | describes what the reader learns about Muhammad Atta as he is portrayed in the excerpt:<br>• considers himself to be radically different from the majority of the people | 2 | |
| 3 | • is attracted by Islamist fundamentalism and the concept of *jihad* without being driven by any religious or political motives | 4 | |
| 4 | • aggressively rejects all worldly things | 2 | |
| 5 | • nihilistic contempt and disapproval of women/sexual pleasures, music, laughter, and even of his fellow terrorists | 2 | |
| 6 | • no belief in life after death/paradisiacal rewards | 2 | |
| | • high level of education (academic degrees, two foreign languages) | 2 | |
| 6 | fulfils another criterion which is related to the task | (2) | |
| | total | 16 | |

## Aufgabe 2 (Analysis) – Anforderungen: The student …

| | | points | |
|---|---|---|---|
| 1 | examines Atta's character and outlines his<br>• aggression towards and contempt of nearly everything secular as well as religious<br>• self-contradictory support of fundamentalism and disapproval of fundamentalist/Islamist issues<br>• atheistic/nihilistic position | 6 | |
| 2 | analyses the point of view and its function in the context of the excerpt:<br>• third-person narration from Atta's point of view<br>• selective use of reported thought (cf. ll. 32–33), enabling the recipient to get an insight into Atta's mind<br>• reader gets to know Atta's interior motivation and is at the same time required to keep a critical distance to the character | 6 | |
| 3 | analyses the syntactical level, e. g.:<br>• repetitions (cf. e.g. ll. 1–2, 6–7, 24–25) and anaphora (cf. e.g. ll. 9–10, 12–13, 36): Atta tirelessly drums fundamentalist issues into himself<br>• enumerations (cf. ll. 4–5, 13–14): all-embracing hatred and spite<br>• contrastive comparison (cf. ll. 13–14): Atta's self-proclaimed outstanding status<br>• combination of paratactic and hypotactic sentences: high level of education, militarist simplicity of Atta's convictions | 8 | |
| 4 | analyses the semantic level, e. g.:<br>• the world as a mere "thing" (ll. 8 and 27): metaphorical debasement of everything secular<br>• use of informal register (cf. l. 29) and words with negative connotations (e.g. "rubbish", l. 15; "sodomy", l. 22): expressions of hatred | 4 | |

| | | | |
|---|---|---|---|
| 5 | fulfils another criterion which is related to the task | (4) | |
| | total | 24 | |

## Aufgabe 3 (Comment) – Anforderungen: The student ...

| | | points | |
|---|---|---|---|
| 1 | explains Atta's role in the terrorist attacks of 9/11 (e.g. one of the leaders of the terrorist attacks; flew the plane which hit the north tower of the WTC; was the head of a terrorist cell in Hamburg) | 5 | |
| 2 | explains how Atta is represented in DeLillo's novel *Falling Man*:<br>● Atta called 'Amir' in *Falling Man*<br>● different stages of his development are mentioned: his academic studies in Hamburg ("On Marienstrasse") and his flight training in Florida ("In Nokomis")<br>● two different types of terrorists: Amir, the convicted fundamentalist leader, and Hammad as his follower, who is temporarily interested in leading a 'normal life'<br>● Hammad as 'main character' of the subplot, not Atta | 10 | |
| 3 | comments on Amis's portrait of the terrorist and its plausibility against this contextual background (e.g. problem of Western approach to Islamist fundamentalism, difficulty of 'reading' the mind of a terrorist) | 5 | |
| 4 | fulfils another aspect which is related to the task | (4) | |
| | total | 20 | |

## Kommunikative Textgestaltung – Anforderungen: Der Prüfling ...

| | | points | |
|---|---|---|---|
| 1 | erstellt einen kohärenten und flüssig lesbaren Text | 5 | |
| 2 | beachtet die Normen der jeweils geforderten Textsorte | 5 | |
| 3 | belegt seine Aussagen durch konkrete Verweise und Zitate | 5 | |
| 4 | strukturiert seinen Text in erkennbare und thematisch kohärente Abschnitte | 5 | |
| 5 | stellt die Gedanken in logischer, folgerichtiger Weise dar und verknüpft diese sinnvoll | 5 | |
| 6 | gestaltet den Text ökonomisch (Vermeidung unnötiger Wiederholungen und Umständlichkeiten) | 5 | |
| | total | 30 | |

## Ausdrucksvermögen/Verfügbarkeit sprachlicher Mittel – Anforderungen: Der Prüfling ...

| | | points | |
|---|---|---|---|
| 1 | formuliert verständlich, präzise und klar | 4 | |
| 2 | bedient sich eines sachlich wie stilistisch angemessenen und differenzierten allgemeinen Wortschatzes | 4 | |
| 3 | bedient sich eines treffenden und differenzierten thematischen Wortschatzes | 4 | |

| | | | |
|---|---|---|---|
| 4 | bedient sich in sachlich wie stilistisch angemessener Weise der fachmethodischen Terminologie | 4 | |
| 5 | bildet komplexe Satzgefüge und variiert den Satzbau | 10 | |
| 6 | löst sich von Formulierungen des Ausgangstextes und formuliert eigenständig | 4 | |
| | total | 30 | |

**Sprachrichtigkeit – Anforderungen: Der Prüfling ...**

| | | points | |
|---|---|---|---|
| | ist in der Lage, einen Text nach den Normen der sprachlichen Korrektheit zu verfassen | 30 | |

| | points | |
|---|---|---|
| **total** | 150 | |

# Konzeption des Unterrichtsmodells

Kaum ein anderes Ereignis in der jüngeren Geschichte der Vereinigten Staaten von Amerika ist in vergleichbar intensiver Form medial aufbereitet und überformt worden wie die Terroranschläge vom 11. September 2001. Dieses Unterrichtsmodell verzichtet zumeist bewusst darauf, auf dieses in der Regel leicht zugängliche reichhaltige Bildangebot zurückzugreifen, und versucht stattdessen, den Text selbst zum Sprechen zu bringen.
Das vorliegende Modell ist so aufgebaut, dass zunächst eine überwiegend eher traditionell ausgerichtete Erarbeitung zentraler Aspekte der Erzähltextanalyse (*character, setting, plot, narrative technique*) auf dem Programm steht, während sich anschließend das Augenmerk verstärkt auf verschiedene für *Falling Man* wie teilweise auch für unsere unmittelbare Gegenwart relevante Kontexte und Themen richtet. Die Gliederung des Unterrichtsmodells folgt, was die ersten drei Bausteine betrifft, inhaltlich der Struktur des Romans. Dementsprechend enthalten diese *Components* jeweils ein Arbeitsblatt zur Sicherung des Textverständnisses, das zugleich in den Bereich der Analyse hineinführt.

Der Schwerpunkt von ***Component 1*** liegt auf dem ersten Teil des Romans („Bill Lawton", Kapitel 1–5) und verfolgt das Ziel, kleinschrittig in die Lektüre einzuführen, die Hauptfiguren kennenzulernen und zentrale Aspekte der Erzähltextanalyse an ausgewählten Passagen einzuüben.

***Component 2*** beschäftigt sich überwiegend mit dem zweiten Teil des Romans („Ernst Hechinger", Kapitel 6–9) und dem Thema des Terrorismus, wobei DeLillos Roman nicht nur islamistisch motivierten Terror in den Fokus rückt, sondern auch Bezüge zu anderen historischen Formen terroristischer Gewalt (RAF, Rote Brigarde) herstellt. Die Schülerinnen und Schüler sollen sowohl Kenntnisse über den politischen Terror der 1970er-Jahre als auch über den religiös-fundamentalistisch motivierten Terror der Gegenwart erwerben bzw. vertiefen, um in die Lage versetzt zu werden, begründet zu Textaussagen Stellung zu nehmen.

***Component 3*** bezieht sich vorrangig auf den dritten Teil des Romans („David Janiak", Kapitel 10–13) und die beiden verwandten Themen Glücksspiel und Aktionskunst, die mit den Figuren Keith Neudecker bzw. dem titelgebenden *Falling Man* assoziiert sind. Dem spielerisch-künstlerischen Schwerpunkt dieses Bausteins entsprechend, kommen verstärkt kreative und handlungsorientierte Methoden zum Einsatz.
Im Mittelpunkt von ***Component 4*** steht das für die Konstruktion des Textes insgesamt nicht minder bedeutsame Thema der (individuellen und kollektiven) Erinnerung, das DeLillo zudem mit der Thematik des demenziell bedingten Vergessens engführt. In diesem Zusammenhang stellt sich schließlich die im Unterricht intensiv zu diskutierende Frage, ob und inwiefern DeLillos Roman die Erinnerung an 9/11 in der Öffentlichkeit gegenwärtig zu halten vermag.

Die in ***Component 5*** vorgestellten Songs zum 11. September bilden nicht den Abschluss der Unterrichtsreihe, sondern sind vielmehr als variable Bausteine aufzufassen, auf die zu verschiedenen Zeitpunkten der Textanalyse zurückgegriffen werden kann, um zwischenzeitlich die fordernde Arbeit an DeLillos komplexen Romangefüge zu unterbrechen und einen anderen, affektiveren Zugang zur Thematik zu ermöglichen.

Component 1

# Approaching the novel: characters, structure and narrative technique

## 1.1 Approaching *Falling Man*

Die Seite *Getting Started* sollte zu Beginn der Unterrichtsreihe auf Folie kopiert werden. Es empfiehlt sich, zunächst das untere Bild auf dem Tageslichtprojektor abzudecken, damit die Schülerinnen und Schüler sich möglichst unvoreingenommen über den (vielbeschworenen) Reiz des Bungee-Jumpings äußern können (Freiheitsgefühl, Risiko, Loslassen, ultimativer Kick durch Grenzerfahrung). Eine erste visuelle Hinführung zum zentralen Thema und Titel des Romans erfolgt mithilfe des zweiten Fotos, der berühmten Momentaufnahme eines der sogenannten *jumpers* aus dem in Flammen stehenden und vom Einsturz bedrohten Nordturm des World Trade Centers, das bezeichnenderweise mit „The Falling Man" betitelt ist. Der Kontrast der beiden Fotos soll eine kognitive Dissonanz provozieren und somit einen Assoziationsprozess in Gang setzen, in dessen Verlauf die Schülerinnen und Schüler ihre Eindrücke und ihr Vorwissen zu den Terroranschlägen vom 11. September 2001 einbringen können, um dabei zugleich für die Lektüre des Romans motiviert zu werden.
Da die Schülerinnen und Schüler am 11. September 2001 im Grundschulalter waren, ist zu Beginn der Reihe zunächst zu klären, ob und inwiefern sie sich überhaupt persönlich an diesen Tag erinnern können und/oder ob diese Erinnerungen bereits durch Äußerungen von Eltern, Lehrern und durch mediale Einflüsse geprägt sind.

How did you/your friends/your parents experience this day?

Anschließend erfolgt ein Brainstorming, das dazu dienen soll, erste Orientierung zu bieten und Wortfelder zu erschließen.

Write down all the words/expressions/ideas you associate with 9/11.

Nachdem die Ergebnisse des Brainstormings von einem Schüler/einer Schülerin zunächst ungeordnet an der Tafel notiert worden sind, gilt es in einem zweiten Schritt, Kriterien zu entwickeln, nach denen die genannten Begriffe geordnet werden können. Das Ergebnis könnte folgendermaßen aussehen:

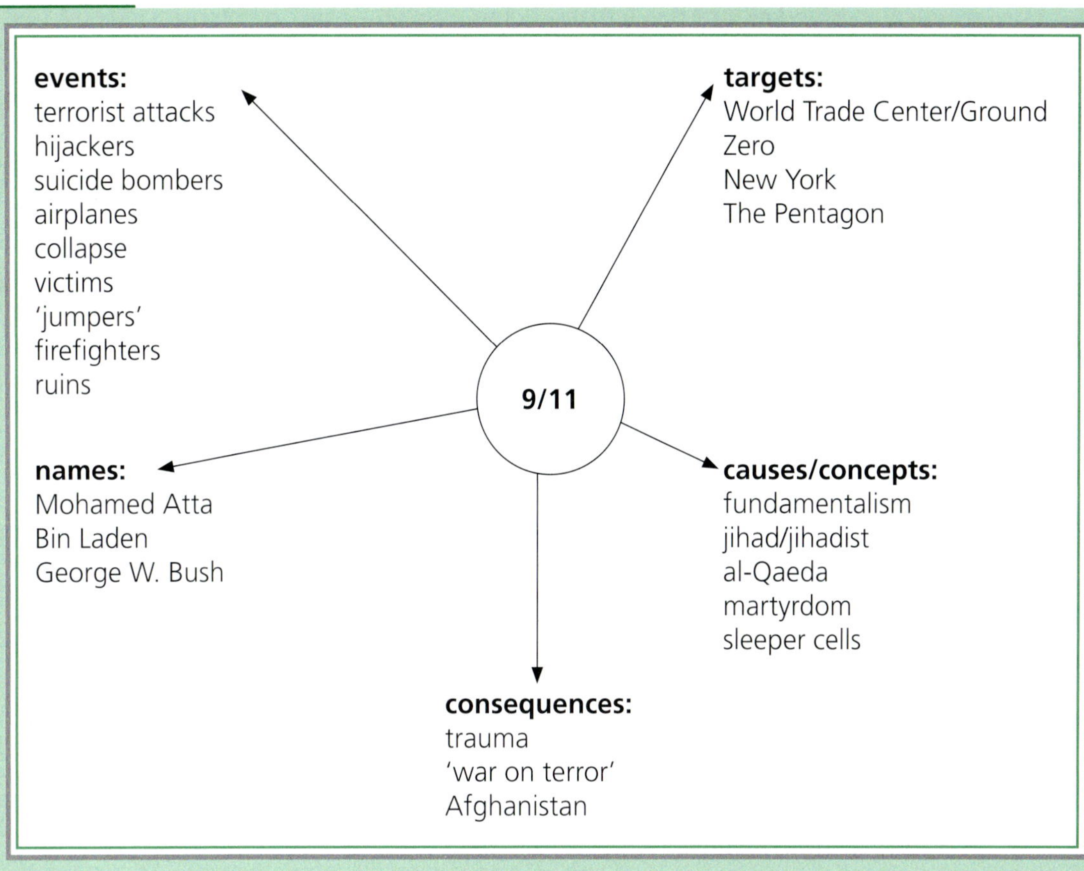


Die Auswertung des Tafelbilds leitet der Lehrer/die Lehrerin mit der bewusst allgemein gehaltenen Frage ein, was an den gesammelten Begriffen auffällt. Da davon auszugehen ist, dass kein einziger Name eines Opfers der Terroranschläge vom 11. September genannt worden ist, zielt die Anschlussfrage darauf ab, auf eben diese signifikante Leerstelle aufmerksam zu machen:

> Why do we know the names of the terrorists and not a single one of the victims?

Bei dem Versuch, Antworten auf diese Frage zu entwickeln, ist darauf zu achten, dass der Roman schließlich selbst ins Spiel gebracht wird, dessen Funktion ja eben darin bestehen könnte, die genannte Leerstelle mit spezifisch literarischen Mitteln zu füllen. Unterhalb des Tafelanschriebs (s. o.) ist deshalb vom Lehrer/von der Lehrerin festzuhalten:

→ no names of victims
→ DeLillo's *Falling Man* may be trying to fill the gap

Um zu gewährleisten, dass die Schülerinnen und Schüler über die wesentlichen Ereignisse, Hintergründe und Folgen der Attentate vom 11. September 2001 informiert sind, können an dieser Stelle längerfristige Referate vergeben werden, für die sich im Verlauf der Reihe verschiedene Anknüpfungspunkte finden lassen. Folgende Referatsthemen sind zu verteilen:

- topic 1: The terrorist attacks of 9/11 – a survey
- topic 2: Al-Qaeda and its (former) leader Osama Bin Laden
- topic 3: America's "war on terrorism"

Zur Einstimmung auf die Lektüre des Romans kann, soweit es das zur Verfügung stehende Zeitkontingent erlaubt, eine weitere *pre-reading activity* erfolgen, die als zwar recht zeitaufwendig, aber durchaus ertragreich einzustufen ist. Alternativ kann aber auch direkt mit der Analyse des Romananfangs begonnen werden (1.2 The first sentence).
Im Mittelpunkt dieser *pre-reading activity* steht das Buch selbst, dessen äußere Bestandteile (*cover and title, blurb, information about the author*) auf ihren jeweiligen Informationsgehalt zu untersuchen sind. Zu Beginn fordert der Lehrer/die Lehrerin die Schülerinnen und Schüler dazu auf, darüber nachzudenken, wie sie selbst vorgehen, wenn sie ein ihnen bislang unbekanntes Buch zur Hand nehmen:

When you pick up a book, what are the first things/elements you look at? And why?

Es schließt sich folgende arbeitsteilige Gruppenarbeit an, wobei die Möglichkeit besteht, das Arbeitsblatt (***Copy 1***) auf Folie zu kopieren und diese in Form von Schnipseln an die einzelnen Gruppen zu verteilen:

Three groups:

First group: Describe the front cover and speculate on the title.

Second group: Read the blurb. What does it tell you about the novel?

Third group: Read the information about the author. What do you get to know about him?

Die Präsentation der Ergebnisse erfolgt in der Weise, dass ausgewählte Gruppen ihre Folienschnipsel nacheinander auf den Tageslichtschreiber legen und vorstellen, bis das Arbeitsblatt komplettiert ist.

**Lösungsvorschläge zu *Copy 1*:**

***cover and title***: combination of two different photos/pictures: the large, coloured picture shows the top of one of the Twin Towers damaged and covered in smoke; the small photo shows a man dressed in a business suit, covered all over with dust, protecting his face with a handkerchief and carrying a briefcase; the ground is full of debris and the man is obviously trying to get away from the area of destruction; the title "Falling Man" is printed in bold red letters and first of all refers to the physical act of falling, but also to the moral/religious 'Fall of Man', and to the fallen ('those who died in battle'), that is, the victims of the terrorist attacks
***blurb***: the novel is about a separated couple after 9/11 and depicts the impact of this experience on them, thereby exploring the effect of the terrorist attacks on the "American psyche" at the same time
***information about the author***: DeLillo was born in New York City in 1936 as a son of Italian immigrants; before starting his career as an author, he worked for an advertising company; his most important works are his award-winning novel *White Noise*, published in 1985, and the voluminous novel *Underworld* (1997); literary critics consider him to be one of America's most important authors

# Looking at the book

| cover and title |
| --- |
| |

| blurb |
| --- |
| |

| information about the author |
| --- |
| |

## 1.2 The first sentence

Im weiteren Verlauf der Doppelstunde steht die Auseinandersetzung mit dem ersten Satz des Romans, an dem sich beispielhaft zentrale sprachliche und motivische Aspekte von DeLillos Darstellung des 11. Septembers aufzeigen lassen. Der Satz kann wahlweise an die Tafel geschrieben oder im Vorfeld auf Folie notiert werden.

Write down your associations and observations concerning the first sentence of *Falling Man*.

"It was not a street anymore but a world, a time and space of falling ash and near night."

Folgende Ergebnisse sind zu erwarten und von einem oder mehreren Schüler/n an der Tafel oder auf der Folie festzuhalten:

- terrorist attacks on the Twin Towers had a universal dimension; they changed the whole world
- effect of dislocation: no sense of time and space anymore
- loss of orientation, total destruction
- "falling ash"/"near night": images of darkness, the apocalypse

In Zusammenhang mit dem zuletzt genannten Aspekt sollte der Lehrer/die Lehrerin den Begriff Konnotation (engl. *connotation*) einführen bzw. wiederholen, um das semantische Potenzial, mit dem DeLillo zu Beginn des Romans arbeitet, angemessen zu erfassen (z. B. das biblische Konzept der Apokalypse, die kulturgeschichtliche Bedeutung der Nacht).

Read chapters one to three. Mark anything you consider important.

## 1.3 The introduction to the protagonist

Die nächste Unterrichtsstunde ist damit zu beginnen, dass den Schülerinnen und Schülern die Möglichkeit eingeräumt wird, ihre ersten Lektüreerfahrungen zu verbalisieren sowie ihre Schwierigkeiten mit dem Text und ihre Fragen sowohl zum Vokabular als auch zum Inhalt zu äußern. Um das Textverständnis zu sichern und erste analytische Beobachtungen formulieren zu können, erhalten die Kursteilnehmerinnen und -teilnehmer ein Arbeitsblatt mit Zitaten (***Copy 2***). Dieses füllen sie in Partnerarbeit aus; anschließend erfolgt eine Besprechung der Ergebnisse. Die Lösungsvorschläge sind so angelegt, dass sie bereits Zusatzaspekte für den Lehrer/die Lehrerin in den Blick nehmen (etwa Leitmotivstrukturen), die nicht in jedem Fall von den Schülerinnen und Schülern zu erwarten sind.

**Lösungsvorschläge zu *Copy 2*:**

1. From the context it becomes clear that Keith hears the collapse of the second tower from which he narrowly escaped; in addition, the expression "second fall" conjures up the biblical (first) "Fall of Man" and the concept of Original Sin.
2. Another description of the collapsing north tower; this time, the personification "him coming down" has the effect that the boundaries of human life and architecture are blurred; moreover, "him coming down" also recalls the *leitmotif* of the "Falling Man."
3. This sentence comes from a conversation Keith's former wife, Lianne, has with her mother, Nina, three days after the attacks about his unexpected return; Nina is sceptical about the possibility of a family reunion and warns Lianne against being too sympathetic; Nina's statement about Keith having lost friends through the attacks is a first hint at his trauma.
4. *Natura morta* means 'still life' and is the title of the paintings by the Italian painter Georgio Morandi, which Lianne's mother owns; the pictures show groupings of bottles and biscuit tins; *Natura morta* becomes another *leitmotif* of DeLillo's novel.
5. When Keith is in the hospital, the doctor tells him about "organic shrapnel", fragments of human flesh and bone from the suicide bomber's body which pierce the skins of surviving people.
6. Lianne meets Isabel, mother of the Siblings, on the street; they talk about the strange behaviour of their children who are always standing at the window of the Siblings' apartment, searching the skies for something; Isabel thinks that "they're not whispering about clouds," but about "a man" (that is, Bin Laden).
7. "Call or fold" are poker terms; "call" means "to equal a bet" and "fold" signifies "to discard one's hand"; Keith is a passionate poker player and was the host of weekly poker nights before the attacks.

# Comprehension: *Falling Man*, chapters 1–3

**Explain the meaning of the seven quotations from chapters one to three by examining their contexts.**

**1)** In time he heard the sound of the second fall. (p. 9, l. 21)

**2)** That was him coming down, the north tower. (p. 10, l. 3)

**3)** "He had friends in there." (p. 14, ll. 11–12)

**4)** *Natura morta*. (p. 16, l. 4)

**5)** "They call this organic shrapnel." (p. 18, ll. 15–16)

**6)** "They're not whispering about clouds." (p. 19, l. 16)

**7)** Call or fold. (p. 29, l. 4)

Da die Schülerinnen und Schüler als Hausaufgabe die ersten drei Kapitel des Romans gelesen haben sollten, müssten sie dazu in der Lage sein, anhand ihrer Anstreichungen zu erschließen, wie Keith Neudecker, der Protagonist von DeLillos Roman, im ersten Kapitel eingeführt wird. Dabei werden sie unweigerlich erneut mit einer der größten Schwierigkeiten bei der Lektüre konfrontiert, die darin besteht, dass DeLillo es sich zum Prinzip gemacht hat, häufig anstelle der Namen lediglich die Pronomina „he" und „she" zu verwenden, ein Verfahren, dessen Funktion in diesem Zusammenhang unbedingt zu thematisieren ist.

Have a closer look at the first chapter. How is the protagonist introduced? Take notes.

Da es sich um eine vergleichsweise anspruchsvolle und für den weiteren Verlauf der Unterrichtsreihe zentrale Fragestellung handelt, empfiehlt es sich, dass die Lehrperson die Ergebnissicherung an der Tafel übernimmt, um ggf. gezielt Nachfragen stellen zu können.

### The introduction to the protagonist

- outward appearance: wears a suit, carries a briefcase, is covered with glass and blood
- walks away from the Twin Towers, notices the destruction around him, hears the sound of the collapsing second tower
- is finally picked up by a truck
- the pronoun "he" replaces the name

➡ anonymity, the character is denied a personal identity, effect of de-individualization
➡ irritation of the reader corresponds to the character's loss of orientation
➡ aspect of generalisation: the character represents a collective human experience

Nachdem das erste Kapitel detailliert erarbeitet worden ist, sind die Schülerinnen und Schüler aufgefordert, die folgenden beiden Kapitel selbstständig zu erschließen. Bei der folgenden Hausaufgabe besteht die Option einer arbeitsteiligen Vorgehensweise.

Browse through chapters two and three again and fill in the grid (*Copy 3*).

**Lösungsvorschläge zu *Copy 3*:**

Chapter 2:
***setting***: Lianne's apartment (three days after the attacks) and Nina's apartment near Fifth Avenue (Monday after the attacks)
***main characters***: Lianne Glenn, Keith's former wife; Nina Bartos, Lianne's mother
***plot***: chapter starts with Lianne's memories of the first happy years of her marriage to Keith; a postcard showing the cover of Shelley's poem *Revolt of Islam* stops her daydreaming; then, Lianne has a conversation with her mother about the fact that Keith came back to her apartment immediately after the attacks

Chapter 3:
***setting***: a hospital in New York City (on 11 September 2001), a street corner, Lianne's apartment, Keith's old apartment near the collapsed Twin Towers (some days after the attacks)

# *Falling Man*, chapters 2 and 3: Setting, main characters, plot

| chapter | setting (place and time) | main characters | plot |
|---|---|---|---|
| 2 | | | |
| 3 | | | |

***main characters***: Keith; Lianne; Isabel, mother of "the Siblings" (Justin's best friends)
***plot***: Keith is being treated in the hospital by a doctor and gets an MRT; cannot refrain from thinking about his friend Rumsey; Lianne meets Isabel on the street, who tells her that Justin and her two children are always standing at the window of their apartment, searching the sky for planes; Keith returns to his old apartment near the collapsed Twin Towers and feels reminded of his weekly poker games, which have come to an abrupt end because of the attacks

## 1.4 Structure and narrative technique

Am Anfang dieser Stunde haben die Schülerinnen und Schüler Gelegenheit dazu, sich über die Ergebnisse ihrer Hausaufgabe (***Copy 3***) in Kleingruppen auszutauschen, um diese anschließend auf Folien vor dem Plenum zu präsentieren. Dabei ist besonders in Zusammenhang mit der Besprechung des dritten Kapitels darauf zu achten, dass jederzeit Fragen und Probleme zum inhaltlichen Verständnis besprochen werden können, die DeLillos spezifisch postmoderne Erzählweise (Zeitsprünge, unklare Angaben zu Handlungszeiten und -orten, *flashbacks*) hervorrufen dürfte. Diese steht im Mittelpunkt der folgenden Unterrichtseinheit, die durch die folgende Frage eingeleitet werden kann:

When looking at your results on the grid, can you think of some general aspects with regard to the structure of the novel and the narrative technique DeLillo employs?

Bei der Ergebnissicherung obliegt es dem Lehrer/der Lehrerin, den Beobachtungen der Schülerinnen und Schüler entsprechende fachwissenschaftliche Begriffe zuzuordnen. Der Begriff *postmodernism* kann an dieser Stelle zumindest genannt und kurz erläutert, wahlweise auch mithilfe eines Kurzreferates in einer der nächsten Stunden vertieft werden:

**Structure and narrative technique in *Falling Man***

- non-linear narration
- multiperspectiveness: changing points of view, mostly between Lianne and Keith
- personal pronouns often replace individual names (loss of identity)

➡ aspects of postmodernism

Ein weiterer Zwischenschritt besteht darin, basale Kategorien der Erzähltextanalyse in Erinnerung zu rufen und an der Tafel festzuhalten.

Whenever we deal with novels/narrative texts in class, what are the basic categories/aspects of analysis we have to consider?

## Novels – aspects of analysis

- characters and constellation of characters
- setting
- point of view
- narrative technique/narrative strategies
- language, stylistic devices
- intention
- background/contexts: biographical, historical, social, cultural, literary

Anschließend erhalten die Schülerinnen und Schüler ein Merkblatt (***Copy 4***), das vorgelesen und bei Bedarf unter Verweis auf andere, bekannte bzw. im Unterricht bereits behandelte Erzähltexte erläutert wird. Mithilfe dieser Informationen sollen sie das folgende Arbeitsblatt (***Copy 5***), auf dem eine ausgewählte kurze Textstelle aus dem ersten Romankapitel abgedruckt ist, bearbeiten, indem sie diese zunächst in Partnerarbeit erzähltechnisch untersuchen, um anschließend im Rahmen eines kreativen Schreibauftrags einen Wechsel der Erzählperspektive (vom *third-person* zum *first-person narrator*) vorzunehmen. Der Versuch, die im zitierten Passus dargestellten Ereignisse aus der Sicht eines unmittelbar betroffenen Ich-Erzählers wiederzugeben, dient weniger dazu, sich mit dem Protagonisten punktuell zu identifizieren, als vielmehr dazu, den Schülerinnen und Schülern bewusst zu machen, wie es DeLillo mithilfe der von ihm verwendeten Erzählperspektive paradoxerweise gelingt, Nähe zur Figur zu schaffen und dabei zugleich Distanz zu wahren.

Fill in the worksheet on point of view and narrative technique (***Copy 5***) with the help of the definitions from the leaflet (***Copy 4***).

**Lösungsvorschläge zu *Copy 5*:**

1. Third-person narrator with limited point of view (Keith's perspective): reader is kept at a distance while sharing Keith's traumatic experience at the same time; indirect characterization (showing technique): focus on Keith's outward appearance from which the reader has to draw conclusions him- or herself; scenic presentation: no structured summary of events, reader is directly confronted with the catastrophic events
2. I was still wearing my business suit and was carrying the briefcase I had picked up during my flight from the north tower. Suddenly, I felt a sharp pain in my face and on the top of my head, probably caused by broken glass. I could taste blood. When I walked past a Breakfast Special sign, I became aware of the fact that city cops and security guards went running by, hands pressed down on gun butts, probably to keep the weapon steady.

Bei der Präsentation der Ergebnisse ist insbesondere darauf zu achten, inwieweit die selbst verfassten Texte sich von der Vorlage unterscheiden (direkter Zugang zur Gedanken- und Gefühlswelt des Protagonisten, erhöhtes Identifikationspotenzial). Abschließend lässt sich begründet darüber spekulieren, warum DeLillo sich gegen die durchaus naheliegende Option, die verstörenden Ereignisse aus der Ich-Perspektive zu erzählen, entschieden hat:

Why do you think did DeLillo not decide on a first-person narrator?

# Aspects of analysis: point of view & narrative technique

## Point of view

1. **Omniscient narrator (unlimited point of view):**
   A narrator with unlimited knowledge tells the story. He knows everything that has ever happened or will happen. He has complete insight into all his characters, their motivations, and feelings. He is not obliged to adhere to the chronology of events, and can employ elements of flashback and anticipation to heighten the tension. He can also move freely among the different locations and events.

2. **Third-person narrator (limited point of view):**
   A narrator with limited knowledge tells the story. He restricts himself to the point of view of one character and presents the whole action through that character's eyes. The reader only learns what that character sees, hears, feels and thinks.

3. **First-person narrator (limited point of view):**
   The narrator is usually one of the characters of the story and her/his knowledge is naturally limited to her/his own thoughts and feelings. The function of narrating the story can also be handed over to different characters in the text:
   a) **"I" as witness:**
   The "I" as witness is a character in his own right within the story. The natural consequence of this narrative form is that the witness has no more than ordinary access to the mental state of others.
   b) **"I" as protagonist:**
   The main character tells her/his own story in the first person. She/he is limited almost entirely to his own thoughts, feelings and perceptions.

## Narrative technique

**Direct characterization (telling technique):**
The narrator or a character in the text tells the reader explicitly what a character is like.

**Indirect characterization (showing technique):**
The reader learns what a character is like by examining and interpreting what a character thinks, says, feels or does, and how she/he behaves towards others.

**Scenic presentation (showing technique):**
The verbal and/or non-verbal action of a character is shown.

**Panoramic presentation (telling technique):**
The narrator tells the reader about what has happened in a certain period of time.

# Point of view and narrative technique in *Falling Man*

"He wore a suit and carried a briefcase. There was glass in his hair and face, marbled bolls of blood and light. He walked past a Breakfast Special sign and they went running by, city cops and security guards running, hands pressed down on gun butts to keep the weapons steady." (p. 7, ll. 14–18)

1. Analyse the passage in terms of narrative technique. Consider these aspects and comment on their function: point of view, direct/indirect characterization, scenic/panoramic presentation, showing/telling technique.

2. Write a free adaptation of the passage from Keith's point of view in the first person singular ('I' as protagonist). Pay special attention to the differences this change of perspective brings about.

Im Rückgriff auf ihre Ergebnisse sind die Schülerinnen und Schüler nun dazu in der Lage, Distanz als für *Falling Man* insgesamt zentrales Prinzip der Erzählhaltung zu benennen.

Read the next two chapters (4 and 5) of the novel.

## 1.5 Constellation of characters

Da die Schülerinnen und Schüler bis zu dieser Stunde nun den gesamten ersten Teil gelesen haben und im Unterricht zur Sprache gekommen ist, wie DeLillo seinen Protagonisten zu Beginn des Textes einführt, sowie weitere Figuren im Rahmen der *while-reading activity* (***Copy 2***) zumindest kurz erwähnt worden sind, geht es nun in einer Einzelstunde darum, sich einen strukturierten Überblick über einen Großteil des Romanpersonals zu verschaffen. Hierzu dient das folgende Arbeitsblatt (***Copy 6***), auf dem in Partner- oder Gruppenarbeit ein Diagramm zur Figurenkonstellation zu entwerfen ist. Eine mögliche Schülerlösung findet sich auf der zweiten Seite des Arbeitsblattes.
Als Präsentationsform eignet sich in diesem Fall besonders gut ein Museumsgang, der so zu organisieren ist, dass die selbstständig gestalteten Diagramme an der Tafel oder einer Wand im Klassenraum befestigt werden, um anschließend den Schülerinnen und Schülern die Möglichkeit zu geben, sämtliche Ergebnisse im direkten Vergleich in Augenschein zu nehmen, zu diskutieren und gegebenenfalls ihren jeweiligen Favoriten zu benennen, der vom Kurslehrer/von der Kurslehrerin nochmals in Kopie für alle Teilnehmer vervielfältigt werden kann.
Die Hausaufgabe aus der Stunde bietet eine wichtige Grundlage zur Charakterisierung der beiden Protagonisten, um die es in der folgenden Stunde geht.

Collect information from the first part of the novel on either Keith or Lianne and take notes.

## 1.6 Writing role biographies of the main characters

Rollenbiografien stellen ein alternatives, bisher vor allem in der Deutschdidaktik weit verbreitetes Verfahren zur traditionellen Form der Figurencharakterisierung dar (vgl. Ingo Scheller, *Szenische Interpretation: Theorie und Praxis eines handlungs- und erfahrungsbezogenen Literaturunterrichts in Sekundarstufe I und II* [Seelze-Velber: Kallmeyer, 2004], S. 61 – 64); die zuletzt genannte Form wird noch in Zusammenhang mit der Figur des fiktiven islamistischen Terroristen Hammad zur Anwendung kommen (2.5 The character of Hammad). Auch und gerade im Fall von *Falling Man*, einem Text, der seinen Leserinnen und Lesern einen direkten Zugang zu den Figuren prinzipiell verweigert, hat das Schreiben von Rollenbiografien in der ersten Person Singular den Vorteil, dass die Schülerinnen und Schüler im Sinne eines Perspektivwechsels aufgefordert sind, sich unmittelbar in eine der beiden Hauptfiguren hineinzuversetzen, um auf diese Weise deren jeweilige Gedanken, Gefühle und persönlichen Erfahrungen, zumal in Bezug auf die Ereignisse vom 11. September, nachzuvollziehen.
Auf der Basis ihrer Notizen, die sie als vorentlastende Hausaufgabe entweder zu Keith oder zu Lianne angefertigt haben, füllen die Schülerinnen und Schüler zunächst in arbeitsteiliger Partnerarbeit, indem sie die auf dem Arbeitsblatt (***Copy 7***) verzeichneten Leitfragen beantworten, eine der beiden Spalten aus. Es folgt der kreative Schreibauftrag, mithilfe der schriftlich fixierten Antworten auf die *guiding questions* in Einzelarbeit eine Rollenbiografie zur gewählten Hauptfigur des Romans anzufertigen. Abschließend stellen einige Freiwillige ihre jeweilige Rolle vor dem Plenum vor bzw. dar, woraufhin sie unbedingt eine Rückmeldung

# Diagram: Constellation of characters in *Falling Man*

Draw a diagram on the basis of the first part of the novel (pp. 7–75) to illustrate the relationships between the following characters: Keith Neudecker, Lianne Glenn, Justin, "the Siblings", Isabel, Nina Bartos, Martin Ridnour, Jack Glenn, Florence Givens, Rosellen S., Falling Man, Bill Lawton.

# Diagram: Constellation of characters in *Falling Man* (possible solution)

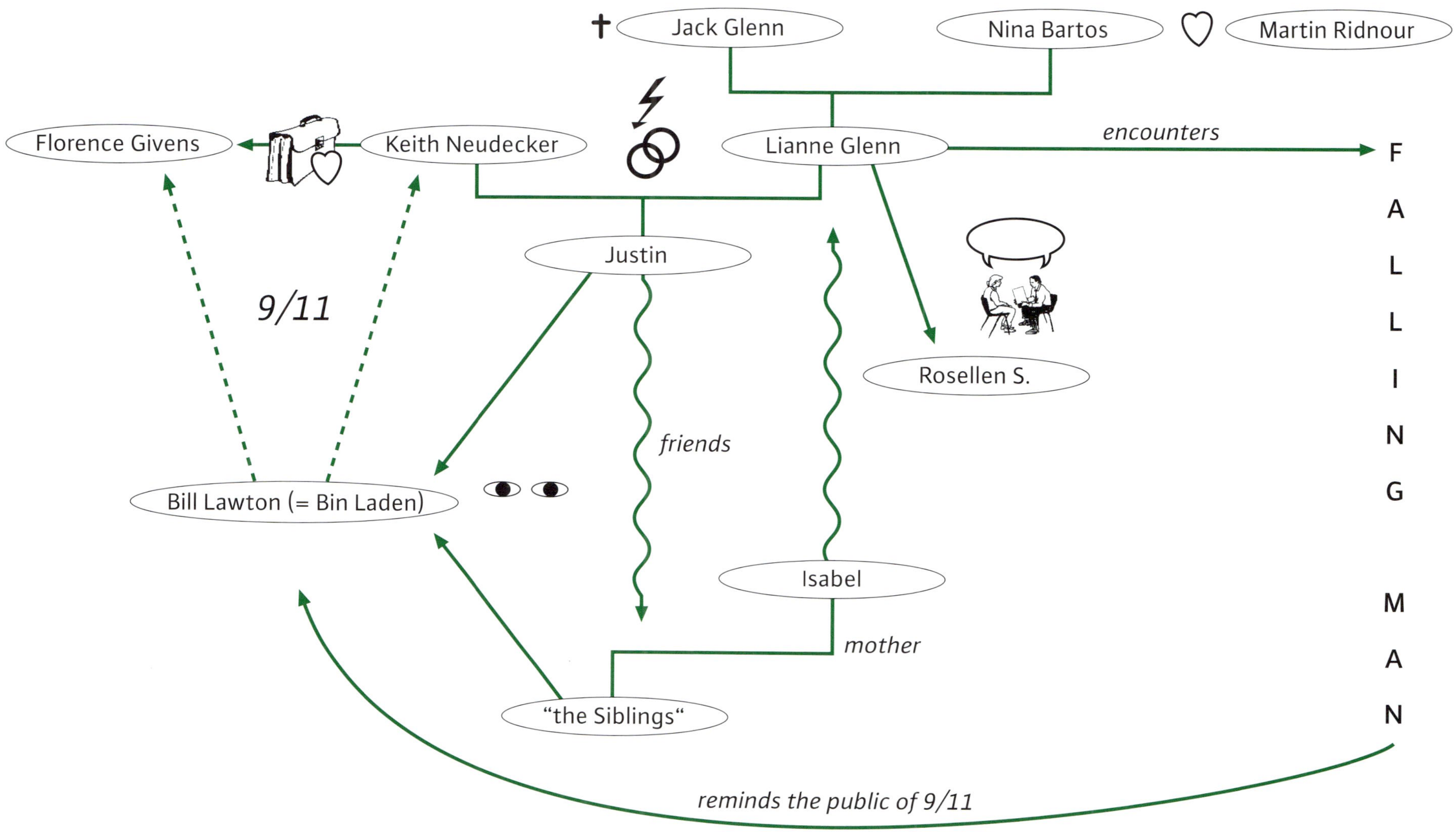

vom Kurs erhalten sollten. Darüber hinaus besteht die Option, besonders gelungene Schülerlösungen für alle zu vervielfältigen.

**Lösungsvorschlag zu *Copy 7*:**

1.

| Guiding questions | Keith Neudecker | Lianne Glenn |
|---|---|---|
| *How old are you?* | thirty-nine, close to forty | thirty-eight, I have been living as a single mother for 1½ years |
| *What is your profession?* | lawyer for a property company (Royer Properties) in the north tower of the WTC | freelance editor for a large publishing company |
| *Who and what is important for you?* | Rumsey, with whom I spent my lunch breaks and did some sports after work; Wednesday poker nights; my wife and child, I have been living apart from them for 1½ years in an apartment near the WTC | my mother and my son; my Alzheimer group; my father Jack Glenn, a former architect, who committed suicide when I was twenty-two (sixteen years ago); Keith |
| *How are your experiences with and your attitude towards family and marriage?* | family experience of separation and alienation, which I do not talk about; affair with Florence Givens, who also survived the attacks | cf. above devastating experience with my own marriage (cf. chapter two); I care a lot about my son and my mother, a former professor of art |
| *Which events in your life shaped your personality?* | I lost two of my friends in the towers; narrow escape from death in the collapsing north tower | my father's suicide; I am convinced I am carrying the same genes and doomed to the same kind of disease |
| *What did you do on 11 September 2001?* | went to work, somehow survived the attacks, then I went to Lianne's apartment, had outpatient surgery at a hospital | when Keith arrived at my apartment, I took him to the hospital; since then, he is living with Justin and me again |

2. Musterlösung ***role biographies***:
My name is **Keith Neudecker** and I am 39 years old. I worked in the World Trade Center as a lawyer for the company Royer Properties until the towers collapsed. Although I managed to escape from the north tower only slightly injured and had to go to a hospital for outpatient surgery, the day changed my life in many ways. I lost two of my best friends, who I used to meet every Wednesday for our weekly poker sessions in my apartment near the towers. In addition, I returned to my wife, Lianne, and my son, Justin, on the day of the attacks after we had been living apart for one and a half years. Lianne and I got married eight years ago, but her mother, Nina Bartos, has always been against our marriage. Although I really tried to make a fresh start with Lianne and Justin after the attacks, I could not help

having an affair with Florence Givens, another survivor of 9/11. I had carried her briefcase home from the towers, and when I found out that she survived, we met and talked about our experiences, finally ending up in bed together.
My name is **Lianne Glenn** and I am 38 years old. I live in an apartment in New York City together with my son, Justin. My profession is freelance editing, but I also voluntarily conduct a self-help group for people suffering from Alzheimer's disease. It is very important for me to do this because my father, Jack Glenn, committed suicide sixteen years ago when he got to know that he had dementia. I am very much afraid of being doomed to this terrible disease, too. On the day of the terrorist attacks, my husband, Keith Neudecker, surprisingly returned to Justin and me after we had been living apart for one and a half years. Keith had been injured in the World Trade Center, and I was very shocked to see him in the doorway of our apartment, covered by glass, blood, and dust. I took him to the hospital where he had to undergo outpatient surgery. At the moment, I do not know if we will be able to be a 'normal' family again. My mother, Nina, is not happy with Keith's return to me because she thinks that his friends are all he cares for. Only time can tell how we will get along with each other and how Keith will cope with his traumatic experiences.

Zur Vorbereitung auf den nachfolgenden Component 2 erhalten die Schülerinnen und Schüler den Auftrag, den zweiten Teil des Romans zu lesen.

Read part two of the novel. Mark anything you consider important.

# Keith and Lianne: role biographies of the main characters

1. Answer the guiding questions on either Keith or Lianne on the basis of your notes.
2. Write a role biography of the character you have chosen to work on. A role biography is **a self-characterization of a fictional character in the first person singular** which serves to present this character to the class.

| Guiding questions | Keith Neudecker | Lianne Glenn |
|---|---|---|
| *How old are you?* | | |
| *What is your profession?* | | |
| *Who and what is important for you?* | | |
| *How are your experiences with and your attitude towards family and marriage?* | | |
| *Which events in your life shaped your personality?* | | |
| *What did you do on 11 September 2001?* | | |

Component 2

# Islamist and communist terrorism – "the same classical pattern"?

Im Mittelpunkt dieser Unterrichtssequenz steht der zweite Teil des Romans, in dem DeLillo anhand der ambivalent konzipierten Figur Martin Ridnour alias Ernst Hechinger in bewusst provokativer Weise Bezüge herstellt zwischen den Attentaten vom 11. September und Formen politisch motivierten Terrors im Europa der Siebzigerjahre (RAF, Rote Brigade).

## 2.1 Defining terrorism and aspects of its history

Bevor der Fokus sich auf die Thematik des Terrorismus richtet, ist es unerlässlich, im Vorfeld zentrale Handlungselemente des zweiten Teils inhaltlich zu sichern. Dies erfolgt in Form einer weiteren Sammlung von Textzitaten (***Copy 8***), die entweder zu Beginn der Stunde in Partnerarbeit oder wahlweise auch als *while-reading activity* in Form einer lektürebegleitenden Hausaufgabe zur Stunde bearbeitet werden kann (s. o.). Bei der Besprechung des Arbeitsblattes sollte es wieder ausreichend Gelegenheit geben, Verständnisfragen inhaltlicher wie sprachlicher Art zu klären, zumal nach dem eher kleinschrittigen Vorgehen in der ersten Unterrichtssequenz die Schülerinnen und Schüler nun erstmals aufgefordert gewesen sind, sich eine größere Textmenge selbstständig zu erschließen.

**Lösungsvorschläge zu *Copy 8*:**

1. When Keith arrives at Lianne's apartment, he is covered with blood, most of it coming from someone else.
2. Florence, the owner of the briefcase Keith has carried along on his flight from the WTC, thinks that Keith has saved her life because she can talk her traumatic experiences over with him; in addition, their love affair has ended her phase of lethargy and shock.
3. Lianne complains about the loudness of the oriental music her neighbour, Elena, listens to all day long; Lianne gets so aggressive that she hits Elena in the face.
4. Rumsey was Keith's closest friend who even confided to Keith that he suffered from the compulsion to count all kinds of things.
5. When Keith accompanies Florence to a shop where she wants to buy a new mattress, he watches two men making racist comments about her; as a result, he hits one of them and even believes himself ready to kill him.
6. "Nineteen" refers to the number of German terrorists belonging to the RAF who are portrayed on a wanted poster of the early seventies; Nina tells Lianne that her lover Martin has been keeping this poster for many years.
7. This refers to the performance artist Lianne meets for the second time after the attacks on the streets of New York City as well as to the title of the novel itself.

# Comprehension: *Falling Man*, part two

**Explain the meaning of the seven quotations from the second part of DeLillo's novel by re-reading and examining their contexts.**

1) Most of it came from somebody else. (p. 87, l. 25)

2) "You saved my life." (p. 107, l. 19)

3) "It's fucking loud." (p. 117, l. 22)

4) He admitted everything, concealed nothing. (p. 118, ll. 22–23)

5) He was angry now. (p. 130, l. 27)

6) "Nineteen." (p. 142, l. 16)

7) Falling man. (p. 158, l. 25)

Nachdem durch eine ausführliche Besprechung der Ergebnisse (***Copy 8***) ein globales Textverständnis sichergestellt worden ist, führt ein visueller Impuls zu einer ersten Annäherung an die prekäre Thematik des Terrorismus (***Copy 9***). Die Schülerinnen und Schüler sehen sich zunächst mit dem oberen Foto konfrontiert; das untere sollte erst einmal abgedeckt werden. Zu sehen sind die RAF-Terroristen Andreas Baader und Gudrun Ensslin auf der Anklagebank vor der Urteilsverkündung im Frankfurter Brandstifter-Prozess im Jahr 1968.

Describe the two persons in the first photo. Do they appear likeable to you? Do you know who they are?

Bei dem Unterrichtsgespräch ist darauf zu achten, dass keine allzu starke Lenkung vonseiten des Kursleiters/der Kursleiterin erfolgt, um positive und identifikatorische Reaktionen nicht von vornherein zu unterbinden. Allerdings ist damit zu rechnen, dass die beiden Terroristen zumindest einzelnen Schülerinnen und Schülern namentlich bekannt sein dürften, da es in der jüngeren Vergangenheit wiederholt filmische Aufarbeitungen des sogenannten Deutschen Herbstes gegeben hat.
Erst nachdem das erste Foto ausführlich besprochen worden ist, erfolgt der zweite visuelle Impuls.

Describe the second picture. Is this poster in any way related to the novel? How?

Bei diesem Poster handelt es sich um ein weiteres historisches Dokument aus den 1970er-Jahren, auf dem insgesamt 19 strafrechtlich verfolgte Mitglieder der RAF im Passbildformat abgebildet sind, unter ihnen auch – an zweiter und dritter Stelle in der ersten Reihe – Andreas Baader und Gudrun Ensslin. Auf die Frage, ob und inwiefern das Poster mit DeLillos Roman in Beziehung zu setzen ist, gibt es eine für die Schülerinnen und Schüler durchaus naheliegende Antwort: Die Anzahl der abgebildeten RAF-Terroristen ist nämlich mit jener identisch, von der in *Falling Man* fast beiläufig die Rede ist, eben „Nineteen" (vgl. ***Copy 8***).
Das zuletzt verwendete Arbeitsblatt hat also auch die Funktion einer inhaltlich-didaktischen Vorentlastung, liefert das fünfte Zitat doch einen Hinweis darauf, dass die fiktive Romanfigur Martin Ridnour eine Kopie des realen Posters besitzt, um dessen Beschreibung es hier geht.
Bevor eine historisch fundierte Annäherung an das emotional hochbesetzte Thema des Terrorismus erfolgt, stellt der Lehrer/die Lehrerin die folgende schülerorientierte Frage:

Are you afraid of terror(ism)?

Nun sind die Schülerinnen und Schüler aufgefordert, in Einzelarbeit den Begriff *terrorism* spontan und selbstständig zu definieren, ohne dabei auf Hilfsmittel (Lexika etc.) zurückgreifen zu können:

What is terrorism? Think of and write down a definition.

Die Ergebnisse werden vorgestellt, miteinander verglichen und schließlich zu der Definition aus der *Encyclopædia Britannica*, die auf dem folgenden Informationsblatt (***Copy 10***) zu finden ist, in Beziehung gesetzt. Die Schülerinnen und Schüler erhalten in Form der insgesamt drei auf dem Blatt zitierten Lexikoneinträge historisches Kontextwissen, das sie in die Lage versetzt, die Konzeption der Figur Martin Ridnour, um die es im folgenden Teil der Stunde gehen wird, besser zu verstehen.

# Anarchistische Gewalttäter
## – Baader/Meinhof-Bande –

**Wegen Beteiligung an <u>Morden, Sprengstoffverbrechen, Banküberfällen und anderen Straftaten</u> werden steckbrieflich gesucht:**

**Meinhof,** Ulrike,
7. 10. 34 Oldenburg

**Baader,** Andreas Bernd,
6. 5. 43 München

**Ensslin,** Gudrun,
15. 8. 40 Bartholomae

**Meins,** Holger Klaus,
26. 10. 41 Hamburg

**Raspe,** Jan-Carl,
24. 7. 44 Seefeld

**Stachowiak,** Ilse,
17. 5. 54 Frankfurt/M.

**Jünschke,** Klaus,
6. 9. 47 Mannheim

**Augustin,** Ronald,
20. 11. 49 Amsterdam

**Braun,** Bernhard,
25. 2. 46 Berlin

**Reinders,** Ralf,
27. 8. 48 Berlin

**Barz,** Ingeborg,
2. 7. 48 Berlin

**Möller,** Irmgard,
13. 5. 47 Bielefeld

**Mohnhaupt,** Brigitte,
24. 6. 49 Rheinberg

**Achterath,** Axel,
15. 4. 35 Hannover

**Hammerschmidt,** Katharina,
14. 12. 43 Danzig

**Keser,** Rosemarie,
24. 8. 47 Ebersberg

**Hausner,** Siegfried,
24. 1. 52 Selb/Bayern

**Brockmann,** Heinz,
1. 3. 48 Gütersloh

**Fichter,** Albert,
18. 12. 44 Stuttgart

**Für Hinweise, die zur Ergreifung der Gesuchten führen, sind insgesamt 100 000 DM Belohnung ausgesetzt, die nicht für Beamte bestimmt sind, zu deren Berufspflichten die Verfolgung strafbarer Handlungen gehört. Die Zuerkennung und die Verteilung erfolgen unter Ausschluß des Rechtsweges.**

**Mitteilungen, die auf Wunsch vertraulich behandelt werden, nehmen entgegen:**

**Bundeskriminalamt – Abteilung Sicherungsgruppe –**
**53 Bonn-Bad Godesberg, Friedrich-Ebert-Straße 1 – Telefon: 02229 / 53001**
**oder jede Polizeidienststelle**

**Vorsicht! Diese Gewalttäter machen von der Schußwaffe rücksichtslos Gebrauch!**

# Terrorism – Definitions from the *Encyclopædia Britannica*

**terrorism**, the systematic use of violence to create a general climate of fear in a population and thereby to bring about a particular political objective. Terrorism has been practiced by political organizations with both rightist and leftist objectives, by nationalistic and religious groups, by revolutionaries, and even by state institutions such as armies, intelligence services, and police.

**Red Army Faction (RAF)**, also called Red Army Fraction, byname Baader-Meinhof Gang, German Rote Armee Fraktion, Baader-Meinhof Gruppe, West German radical leftist group formed in 1968 and popularly named after two of its early leaders, Andreas Baader (1943–77) and Ulrike Meinhof (1934–76).

From its early years, members of the Red Army Faction supported themselves through bank robberies and engaged in terrorist bombings and arson, especially of West German corporations and businesses and of West German and U.S. military installations in West Germany. They also kidnapped and assassinated prominent political and business figures. By the mid-1970s, the group expanded its scope outside West Germany and occasionally allied itself with militant Palestinian groups. For example, in 1976 two Baader-Meinhof guerrillas took part in a Palestinian hijacking of an Air France jetliner, which eventually ended after the successful Entebbe raid in Uganda by Israeli commandos.

The Red Army Faction included at least 22 core members in the early 1970s, most of whom, including Meinhof, had been jailed by the summer of 1972. Baader, escaping one imprisonment in 1970, was arrested again in 1976. Meinhof hanged herself in her cell in 1976. Three others, including Baader, were found shot dead in their cells on October 18, 1977. Ostensibly suicides, their deaths came one day after West German commandos stormed a hijacked Lufthansa plane in Mogadishu, Somalia, blocking the hijackers' attempt to win the release of their jailed comrades as ransom for their hostages. […] The group formally disbanded in 1998, though arrests and trials continued.

**Red Brigades**, Italian Brigate Rosse, militant left-wing organization in Italy that gained notoriety in the 1970s for kidnappings, murders, and sabotage. Its self-proclaimed aim was to undermine the Italian state and pave the way for a Marxist upheaval led by a "revolutionary proletariat." […] Between 1974 and 1988, the Red Brigades carried out about 50 attacks, in which nearly 50 people were killed. A common nonlethal tactic employed by the group was "kneecapping," in which a victim was shot in the knees so that he could not walk again.

At its height in the 1970s, the Red Brigades was believed to comprise 400 to 500 full-time members, 1,000 members who helped periodically, and a few thousand supporters who provided funds and shelter. Careful, systematic police work led to the arrest and imprisonment of many of the Red Brigades' leaders and ordinary members from the mid-1970s onward, and by the late 1980s the organization was all but destroyed. However, a group claiming to be the Red Brigades took responsibility in the 1990s for various violent attacks, including those against a senior Italian government adviser, a U.S. base in Aviano, and the NATO Defense College.

(*Encyclopædia Britannica Online*, http://www.britannica.com)

**intelligence services** secret service for obtaining information of military or political value

**arson** the act of wilfully setting fire to another man's property

**assassinated** killed

**guerrillas** people engaged in an irregular war

**raid** a surprise visit by police to arrest suspects

**ostensibly** declaredly

**ransom** a sum of money paid to obtain pardon for an offence

**notoriety** being known in a negative sense

**nonlethal** not deadly

## 2.2 The character of Martin Ridnour/Ernst Hechinger

Nachdem die Thematik des politisch motivierten Terrorismus der Sechziger- und Siebzigerjahre allgemein behandelt worden ist, gerät nun die zwielichtige Figur Martin Ridnour alias Ernst Hechinger ins Zentrum des Interesses. Durch die folgende Partnerarbeit lassen sich die wichtigsten Informationen zu dieser Figur zusammentragen:

Re-read p. 139, l. 20 – p. 144, l. 17. What do you get to know about Martin Ridnour in this passage? Take notes.

Die Sicherung der Ergebnisse erfolgt entweder durch den Lehrer/die Lehrerin oder durch einen Schüler/eine Schülerin an der Tafel:

**Martin Ridnour**

- Nina and he have known each other for twenty years
- profession: art investor/art dealer
- his real name is Ernst Hechinger
- he is married to another woman
- at their first meeting, Nina told him about the artist Giorgio Morandi
- Nina suspects him of having dealt in stolen goods
- he was a member of the German collective Kommune One in the late 1960s
- he was possibly involved in the activities of the Red Brigades in Italy
- keeps a wanted poster of the nineteen RAF terrorists in his apartment in Berlin
- he thinks that the jihadists and their visions of brotherhood are similar to the radicals of the sixties and seventies

Es folgt eine vorentlastende Hausaufgabe, auf deren Grundlage in der folgenden Stunde die Position Ridnours/Hechingers zur Vergleichbarkeit des gegenwärtigen islamistischen und des politischen Terrors im Europa der Sechziger- und Siebzigerjahre, die zugleich eine wichtige These des Romans ist, fundiert perspektiviert und diskutiert werden kann:

What exactly does the term "jihadist" mean and where does it come from? Take notes.

## 2.3 Comparing terrorism then and now

Die Einzelstunde beginnt mit der Hausaufgabe zur Stunde, der Klärung der Bezeichnung „jihadist", einer Ableitung des aus dem Arabischen stammenden Begriffs „jihad". Der *Encyclopædia Britannica* sind unter anderem die folgenden Informationen zu entnehmen:

> jihad, also spelled jehad, ("struggle," or "battle"), a religious duty imposed on Muslims to spread Islam by waging war; jihad has come to denote any conflict waged for principle or belief and is often translated to mean "holy war." Islam distinguishes four ways by which the duty of jihad can be fulfilled: by the heart, the tongue, the hand, and the sword.
>
> (Quelle: *Encyclopædia Britannica Online*, http://www.britannica.com)

Im Rückgriff auf Ergebnisse aus der vorangegangenen Stunde zur Charakterisierung der Figur Martin Ridnour alias Ernst Hechinger lässt sich die folgende Frage zur Überleitung stellen:

What does Martin Ridnour alias Ernst Hechinger think about the jihadists of 9/11?

Diese Frage zielt direkt auf die provokative Äußerung ab, dass sich die Attentäter vom 11. September und die linksextremistischen Terroristen der Siebzigerjahre durch vergleichbare Denk- und Verhaltensmuster auszeichnen ("the same classical pattern"). Im Sinne des Anforderungsbereichs III (*Comment*) sollen die Schülerinnen und Schüler diese These mithilfe des folgenden Arbeitsblattes möglichst kontrovers in Kleingruppen diskutieren (***Copy 11***), indem sie zunächst Pro- und Kontraargumente sammeln.

**Lösungsvorschläge zu *Copy 11*:**

***Pros***: both groups are convinced that they bring about necessary changes; they think that they are fighting for a just and important cause; both groups share an experience of community and brotherhood apart from all the others; their proclaimed enemy in both cases is modern capitalist Western society; they do not refrain from using the most violent means (murder, hijacking, bomb attacks); both the RAF and the terrorists of 9/11 are associated with Germany
***Cons***: jihadists follow fundamentalist religious principles whereas the terrorists of the sixties and seventies were driven by leftist, radical Marxist ideology; suicide attacks and martyrdom are essential features of the jihadists, who believe in being eventually rewarded for their deeds, in contrast to the political radicals from Europe, who are mostly atheists; the terrorists of 9/11 wanted to kill as many people as possible whereas the European organisations often attacked or assassinated single representatives of the system they wanted to abolish

Ausgewählte Pro- und Kontraargumente können nach einer längeren Arbeits- und Diskussionsphase auch noch einmal vor dem Plenum vorgetragen werden, sodass anschließend jeder einzelne Schüler und jede einzelne Schülerin selbstständig eine sachlich fundierte, individuelle Schlussfolgerung ziehen kann (vgl. ***Copy 11***). Auch hier sollten kontroverse Schülermeinungen vorgetragen und eventuell erneut diskutiert werden.

Collect information from the internet on the terrorists of 9/11.

## 2.4 Who was Mohamed Atta?

Als visueller Impuls zum Einstieg in die Unterrichtssequenz (***Copy 12***), in deren Mittelpunkt DeLillos Darstellung einiger Attentäter vom 11. September steht, dient ein Foto, auf dem der Wohnort der Hamburger Terrorzelle um Mohamed Atta zu sehen ist. Atta, in *Falling Man* Amir genannt, war der mutmaßliche Pilot jenes Flugzeugs, das im Nordturm des World Trade Centers zerschellte.
Die Schülerinnen und Schüler sind aufgefordert, das auf den ersten Blick vollkommen alltäglich und harmlos wirkende Foto zu beschreiben und Hintergrundinformationen zu diesem Ort einzubringen, auf die sie im Rahmen ihrer häuslichen Recherche zu den Attentätern vom 11. September gestoßen sein können.

Describe what you see. What do you know about this place?

# Terrorism then and now: "the same classical pattern"?

"[Martin] thinks these people, these jihadists, he thinks they have something in common with the radicals of the sixties and seventies. He thinks they're all part of the same classical pattern. They have their theorists. They have their visions of world brotherhood." (p. 142, ll. 24–27)

Do you agree with this position? Find and note down arguments for and against Martin Ridnour's/Ernst Hechinger's view against the background of what you know about the German and Italian "radicals of the sixties and seventies" (RAF, Kommune I, Red Brigades) on the one hand, and the terrorists of 9/11 on the other hand.

| Pros | Cons |
|---|---|
| | |

My conclusion:

# Mohamed Atta – some dates and facts

- grows up in Egypt as the son of a lawyer and a homemaker
- his family and friends describe him as a shy, unassuming young man
- his school friends do not remember ever having seen him pray
- graduates from Cairo University with a degree in architectural engineering
- autumn 1992: Atta enrolls at the Technical University of Hamburg-Harburg where he hopes to earn a degree in urban planning and then return to Egypt
- mid-'90s: Atta begins disappearing from school for extended periods
- in his thesis he explores the conflict between Islam and modernity as reflected in city planning
- from mid-1997 to October 1998: Atta seems to have disappeared from Hamburg entirely
- returns to school with a bushy beard favoured by fundamentalists
- publicly spreads the words of the Koran
- early in 1999: university officials give him permission to found an Islamic student group
- at the end of 1999: Atta, Al-Shehhi and Jarrah report their passports stolen, possibly to clear any record of travel to Afghanistan
- spring 2000: Atta, now clean-shaven, is seen walking into a U. S. Department of Agriculture office in Homestead, Florida
- June 2000: Atta and Al-Shehhi sign up for flight training at Huffman Aviation International in Venice, Florida
- Atta and Al-Shehhi move into a little pink house in Nokomis
- December 21, 2000: Atta and Al-Shehhi get their pilot licenses
- about a week later: three-hour-training on the Boeing 727 simulator at Simcenter Inc. at Opa-Locka Airport, outside Miami
- June 29, 2001: travels to Las Vegas, where he meets with two other hijackers, Salem Alhazmi and Hani Hanjour
- September 7, 2001: Atta, Al-Shehhi and another man visit Shuckum's Oyster Bar and Grill in Hollywood, Florida; he is the only one not to drink any alcohol
- September 11, 2001: Atta is the pilot of the plane that hits the north tower of the World Trade Center, only a few days after his 33rd birthday
- his father, Mohammed El Amir, denies that his son was involved in the attacks ("He is a moderate in his adherence to his faith like me and his mother.")

based on: John Cloud, "Atta's Odyssey", *Time*, Sunday, 30 September 2001 (http://www.time.com/printout/0,8816,176917,00.html)

Nachdem die Schülerinnen und Schüler die Ergebnisse ihrer Internetrecherche mündlich vorgestellt haben, gibt der Kursleiter/die Kursleiterin ihnen in Form eines Informationsblattes zu Mohamed Attas Biografie (***Copy 13***) eine Materialgrundlage an die Hand, mit deren Hilfe sie ihre erworbenen Erkenntnisse zu den Attentätern des 11. September ergänzen und vertiefen. Das Informationsblatt soll die Schülerinnen und Schüler darüber hinaus in die Lage versetzen zu erkennen, wie präzise DeLillo für seinen Roman recherchiert hat, da er sich nachweislich bei der Gestaltung der Figuren Amir und Hammad an zentralen Fakten orientiert hat.

Which of the facts about Mohamed Atta does DeLillo refer to in his novel? Mark them on your copy and look for passages in *Falling Man* (pp. 77–83, 165–172) which are related to these facts. Take notes.

Auf der Grundlage einer erneuten Lektüre der beiden Kapitel „On Marienstraße" und „In Nokomis" lassen sich folgende Informationen über die beiden Figuren Amir und Hammad, die allesamt auf Fakten beruhen (vgl. ***Copy 13***), an der Tafel zusammentragen:

**The terrorists of 9/11: biographical facts in *Falling Man***

- group of terrorists lived in a flat on Marienstraße (Hamburg)
- they grew beards while being in Hamburg
- they were students of architecture and engineering
- Amir's full name was Mohamed Mohamed el-Amir el-Sayed Atta
- Amir (Mohamed Atta) led the discussions
- they went to Internet cafés and learned about flight schools in the U.S.
- they moved into a pink house in Nokomis (Florida)
- attendance of a flight school in Florida
- they were clean-shaven in Nokomis

## 2.5 The character of Hammad

Im weiteren Verlauf der Doppelstunde richtet sich der Fokus auf Hammad, neben Keith Neudecker und Lianne Glenn der dritte Protagonist von DeLillos *Falling Man*, dessen Entwicklung vom partiell westlich orientierten Hamburger Studenten zum fanatisierten Mitläufer und (fiktiven) Mitattentäter der Anschläge auf das World Trade Center drei Teilkapitel der einzelnen Romanabschnitte gewidmet sind. Während die Konzeption der Figur Amir (Mohamed Atta) sowie die im Text erwähnten Stationen der Nebenhandlung im Wesentlichen auf Fakten beruhen, wie im ersten Teil der Doppelstunde deutlich gemacht worden ist, unternimmt DeLillo am Beispiel von Hammad den Versuch, in die Erlebnis-, Gedanken- und Gefühlswelt eines islamistischen Terroristen vorzudringen. Zur Erschließung dieser Figur bietet sich die traditionelle Form der Charakterisierung an, weshalb die Schülerinnen und Schüler zunächst aufgefordert sind, entsprechende Analysekriterien zu benennen:

If you want to characterize a figure like Hammad, which aspects do you have to consider?

Die Ergebnisse gilt es in Form einer Mindmap an der Tafel festzuhalten:

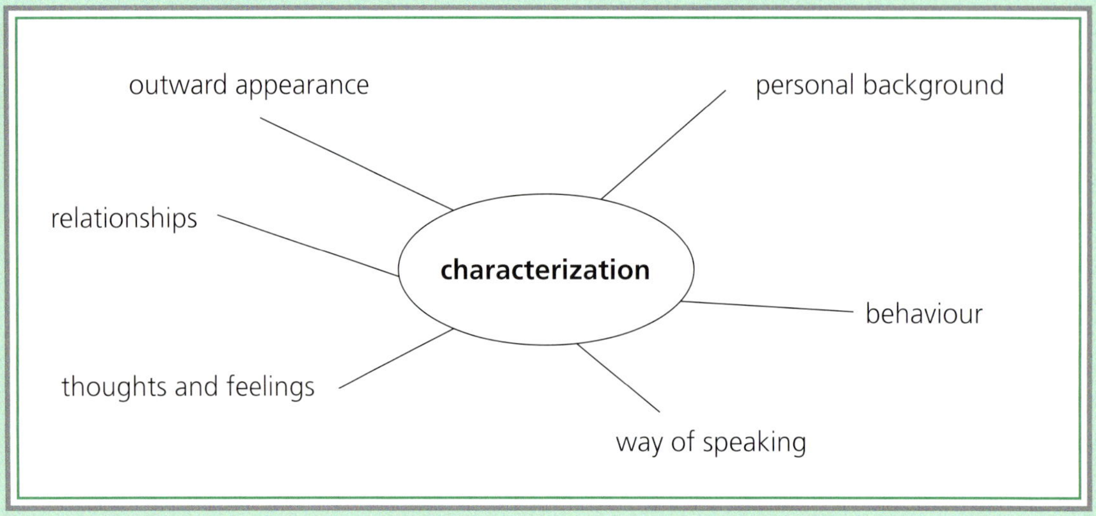


Die im Unterrichtsgespräch zusammengetragenen Aspekte finden sich (mit Ausnahme von *way of speaking*) auf dem Arbeitsblatt (***Copy** 14*) wieder, das die Schülerinnen und Schüler erhalten, um es in Partnerarbeit auszufüllen. Je nach Kursgröße und Zeitkontingent besteht methodisch die Option, arbeitsteilig vorzugehen und jeden einzelnen der fünf auf dem Arbeitsblatt verzeichneten Aspekte als Folienschnipsel zu verteilen. Die fünf Schnipsel lassen sich in der Präsentationsphase wieder zu einem komplett ausgefüllten Arbeitsblatt zusammenfügen, sodass die Schülerinnen und Schüler ihrerseits die jeweils nicht von ihnen bearbeiteten Aspekte auf ihrem eigenen Arbeitsblatt nachtragen können.

**Lösungsvorschlag zu *Copy 14*:**

***outward appearance***: bulky, clumsy, is growing a beard which he is not allowed to trim, loses twenty-two kilos in a training camp in Afghanistan, starts shaving again in Florida, does not change his clothes (T-shirt, cotton trousers) any longer because he has stopped caring about his outward appearance
***background***: comes from the Middle East (country not mentioned), studies either architecture or engineering in Hamburg
***whereabouts***: has been living in a flat on Marienstrasse (Hamburg) together with other Islamists for ten years; then goes to a training camp in Afghanistan; finally moves into a house in Nokomis (Florida) where he attends a flight school
***relationships***: has a love relationship with Leyla, who is German, Syrian and Turkish; goes regularly to a mosque where he meets a man who fought in the Iraq-Iran War in the 1980s; is impressed by the rhetorical skill of Amir (Mohamed Atta), who leads the group of fundamentalists Hammad belongs to and agitates against Jews and Americans; regards Amir as a philosopher; ends all contact with his parents while being in Florida
***thoughts and attitudes***: typical 'follower', is not totally averse to Western lifestyle at the beginning; is interested in women and sexuality; does only inwardly question the radical thinking and the brutal deeds of the others; does not refrain from using physical violence himself; his most important experience in Afghanistan is that he is given a long knife with

# A characterization of Hammad

**Fill in the information on Hammad as he is presented in the chapters "On Marienstraße" and "In Nokomis".**

| | |
|---|---|
| outward appearance | |
| background | |
| whereabouts | |
| relationships | |
| thoughts and attitudes | |

which he has to kill a camel in front of the others; in Florida he is not as good as Amir at the flight school; does not pay women for sex like other members of the group; believes in the concept of martyrdom and regards Amir as a model although he continues to reflect upon leading a 'normal' life

Die Hausaufgabe besteht darin, auf der Basis des ausgefüllten Arbeitsblatts eine ausformulierte Charakterisierung der Figur Hammad anzufertigen.

Write a characterization of Hammad as he is presented in the chapters "On Marienstraße" and "In Nokomis".

Component 3

# The role of gambling and the art of falling

Wie der Titel dieser *Component* bereits signalisiert, geht es im ersten Teil der folgenden Unterrichtssequenz um die Thematik des mit der Figur Keith Neudecker assoziierten Glücks- bzw. genauer Pokerspiels, die sich im Gegensatz zu den ersten beiden Einheiten besonders schülergerecht aufbereiten lässt. Der zweite Teil ist dem titelgebenden Motiv des "Falling Man" gewidmet.

## 3.1 Gambling/playing games

Nach einer ausführlichen Besprechung der Hausaufgabe (s. o.) erfolgt der Einstieg in den neuen Themenkomplex erneut über einen visuellen Impuls (***Copy 15***). Auf der Folie befinden sich zwei Abbildungen; zum einen das Rad der Fortuna (*Wheel of Fortune*), ein aus der Antike stammendes und im Mittelalter weitverbreitetes Motiv, das unter anderem durch Carl Orffs Vertonung der *Carmina Burana* einen großen Bekanntheitsgrad erlangt hat. Mit diesem Motiv sind Schicksalsvorstellungen verknüpft, denen zufolge die Göttin Fortuna durch das Drehen des Rades Menschen entweder zu großem Ruhm verhelfen oder sie plötzlich ins Unglück stürzen kann. Auf der Abbildung ist in der Mitte die Göttin selbst zu sehen, während die Außenseite des Rades verschiedene Schicksalsstationen eines Königs zeigt: Aufstieg (*regnabo* = ich werde regieren; von lat. *regnare* = regieren), Inthronisierung (*regno* = ich regiere), Fall (*regnavi* = ich habe regiert/die Krone verloren) und Niedergang (*sum sine regno* = ich habe keine Macht mehr). Das zweite Foto zeigt eines der zahlreichen Casinos, die das Stadtbild von Las Vegas prägen und den Ruf dieser Metropole als Spielerhochburg mitbegründet haben.
Mittels einer offen gehaltenen Einstiegsfrage lässt sich eruieren, welche Assoziationen die Schülerinnen und Schüler mit den Bildern verbinden:

> What do you see in these two pictures?

Der nächste Schritt besteht zum einen darin, zu verdeutlichen, welche Verbindung zwischen den beiden Bildern auszumachen ist, zum anderen darin, Bezüge zwischen den Abbildungen, insbesondere dem dargestellten Casino, und dem Roman herzustellen.

> To what extent are these pictures related to each other and how are they related to the novel?

Was die beiden Bilder miteinander verbindet, ist die semantische Verknüpfung von ‚Glück' und ‚Spiel'. Diese spiegelt sich unter anderem konkret darin wider, dass das *Wheel of Fortune* (auch *Big Wheel* oder *Money Wheel* genannt) eine in den USA weitverbreitete Form des Glücksspiels ist und darüber hinaus an die Drehscheibe im Roulette erinnert. Beide Bilder lassen sich in Bezug setzen zu Keith Neudeckers Pokerrunden, die im dritten Teil des Romans in Las Vegas ihre Fortsetzung erfahren.

Regno
regnabo
regnavi
sum sine regno
EXALTATUS·FORTUNE·ROTA·VOLVITUR·DESCENDO·MINORATUS·ALTER·IN·ALTUM·TOLLITUR·NIMIS·

DUNES
THE COMEDY
OASIS
CASINO
SOUVENIR PHOTO FREE

# Questionnaire: Gambling/playing games

**1) How often do you gamble/play games in your free time?**

almost every day ☐ more than once per week ☐

more than once per month ☐ less than once per month ☐

once or more often in six months ☐ once a year ☐ never ☐

**2) What kind of games do you like/play?**

card games: ____________________

parlour games: ____________________

board games: ____________________

computer games: ____________________

other kinds: ____________________

**3) Do you play for money?**

yes ☐ no ☐ rarely ☐

**4) My favourite game is**

____________________

**5) Where do you like to gamble/play games?**

____________________

**6) With whom do you gamble/play games?**

____________________

**7) Why do you gamble/play games?**

____________________

Nach diesem eher theoretischen Einstieg erfolgt eine schülerorientierte Phase, in deren Verlauf die Schülerinnen und Schüler über ihr eigenes Spielverhalten reflektieren sollen.

Who likes to gamble/play games?

Um die Antworten auf diese Frage präzisieren und systematisch erfassen zu können, erhalten die Schülerinnen und Schüler einen Fragebogen, den sie in Einzelarbeit ausfüllen (***Copy 16***). Daraufhin findet eine Auswertung der Ergebnisse statt, bei der ein Kursteilnehmer/eine Kursteilnehmerin den Fragebogen mündlich durchgeht und auf einer Folie die Anzahl und Arten der jeweiligen Antworten notiert.

## 3.2 The role of poker in *Falling Man*

Es besteht die Option, entweder zu Beginn oder am Ende der Stunde im Klassenraum eine Runde Poker zu spielen, da Poker sich unter Schülerinnen und Schülern erfahrungsgemäß großer Beliebtheit erfreut und es sich hierbei um ein Spiel handelt, dessen Vokabular im Wesentlichen aus dem Englischen stammt.

What do you know about poker?

Mit dieser Frage verbindet sich die Absicht, entsprechendes Vorwissen abzurufen, um auf diese Weise zugleich die Thematik des Poker- bzw. generell Kartenspiels semantisch zu erschließen. Grundlegendes Vokabular wie etwa das unten genannte gilt es schriftlich festzuhalten:

**Playing cards**

ace/king/queen/jack
four suits: diamonds, hearts, spades, clubs
a deck of cards (cf. Keith Neu**deck**er, a telling name)
(to) riffle/shuffle
(to) deal (out) cards

Das an der Tafel gesammelte Vokabular bildet das semantische Rüstzeug für die folgende Unterrichtsphase, in deren Verlauf die Frage zu beantworten ist, inwiefern das Pokerspiel für DeLillos Roman und dessen Protagonisten von Bedeutung ist. Auch wenn die Schülerinnen und Schüler den dritten Teil des Romans zu diesem Zeitpunkt noch nicht gelesen haben (müssen), sind sie auf der Grundlage ihrer Kenntnisse der ersten beiden Teile dazu in der Lage, die folgende Frage zu beantworten:

What does poker mean to Keith Neudecker?

Mit dieser Frage leitet der Lehrer/die Lehrerin zum textanalytischen Teil der Doppelstunde über, in dem die Schülerinnen und Schüler sich in Partnerarbeit mit den zentralen Stellen des Romans beschäftigen, in denen Keiths Verhältnis zum Pokerspiel thematisiert wird.

Read the following passages. Take notes.
Part one, chapter 3:
p. 28, l. 24 – p. 29, l. 17
Part two, chapter 6:
p. 95, l. 24 – p. 99, l. 25
Part three, chapter 11:
p. 189, l. 1 – p. 190, l. 6

Auf der Grundlage der mündlich präsentierten Ergebnisse könnte sich das folgende Tafelbild ergeben:

**The importance of poker for Keith**

- before the attacks: poker as "the one uncomplicated interval of his week" (p. 29, l. 2)
- played with five other men, among them his closest friend Rumsey
- Keith likes the challenge and the different, 'male' form of communication
- "self-imposed restriction" (p. 98, l. 5): no food, no beer that is not dark, no talk about other subjects, only five-card stud
- importance of friendship (as reflected in the story of the German card players)
- after the attacks: Keith spends most of his time in Las Vegas and gets addicted to the game

Da in Zusammenhang mit der Thematik des Pokerspiels ein punktueller Vorgriff auf den dritten und letzten Teil des Romans erfolgt ist, liegt es nun nahe, diesen Teil in Gänze zu Hause lesen zu lassen.

Read the third part.

## 3.3 Falling Man: the character of David Janiak

Es empfiehlt sich, die Besprechung des dritten Teils von *Falling Man* mit einer weiteren Übung zum Textverständnis zu beginnen (***Copy 17***), wie sie in analoger Form bereits in Zusammenhang mit den ersten beiden Teilen des Romans vorgenommen worden ist. Auch in diesem Fall erhält der Erwartungshorizont für den Lehrer/die Lehrerin relevante Zusatzaspekte.

**Lösungsvorschläge zu *Copy 17*:**

1. Nina Bartos, Lianne's mother, died four months ago; Lianne meets Martin Ridnour alias Ernst Hechinger at the funeral again.
2. Keith now spends most of his time in the hotels and casinos of Las Vegas and has become a professional poker player; although he meets his former friend Terry Cheng from time to time, Keith has become very withdrawn and indifferent, staring into the artificial waterfall of the hotel lobby for hours.
3. Lianne voices her suspicion that Keith wants to kill someone; she has

sensed his inner state of restlessness and aggression after 9/11 but is not able to guess his feelings because he is hiding them from her.

4. This is Lianne's comment on the widely known authentic photo, taken after the attacks, of a man who jumps from the WTC; the metaphor of the "fallen angel" alludes to the biblical figure of Satan, who used to be an angel in heaven but was dispelled from it when he started revolting against God; another indirect reference to the title of the novel.
5. Lianne develops a habit of going to church again in order to cope with her fear of death and the traumatic experience of the terrorist attacks.
6. The last chapter of the book, "In the Hudson Corridor," shows the situation on board the plane which is about to hit the north tower of the WTC; Hammad has been cut by a box cutter accidentally by one of his fellow terrorists in the struggle with the pilot and crew of the plane.
7. The very end of the novel finally reveals how Keith experienced the attacks on the WTC himself; when he realizes that he cannot rescue the mortally wounded Rumsey, he mechanically grasps the briefcase during his flight from the north tower, which turns out to belong to Florence Givens.

Mit David Janiak, jenem fiktiven Aktionskünstler, dem Lianne Glenn nach den Anschlägen vom 11. September 2001 in New York City wiederholt zufällig begegnet, gerät im weiteren Verlauf dieser Stunde eine Figur in den Blick, die für den Roman, dessen Titel *Falling Man* bereits auf sie verweist, von durchaus zentraler Bedeutung ist. In der Absicht, eine erste Annäherung an diese Figur zu ermöglichen, erkundigt sich der Lehrer/die Lehrerin nach den titelgebenden Namen der drei Romanteile, um den Schülerinnen und Schülern auf diese Weise zugleich die Makrostruktur des Textes vor Augen zu führen:

What are the titles of the three parts of *Falling Man*? What do these names stand for?

Aus den Antworten ergibt sich folgendes Tafelbild:

**The three parts of *Falling Man***

| | | |
|---|---|---|
| Part I: Bill Lawton | ➜ | Osama Bin Laden |
| Part II: Ernst Hechinger | ➜ | Martin Ridnour |
| Part III: David Janiak | ➜ | "Falling Man" |

Da die Identität der beiden ersten titelgebenden Figuren im Unterricht bereits geklärt worden ist, stellt sich nun die Frage, um wen es sich bei David Janiak nun eigentlich genau handelt.

What do you know about David Janiak?

# Comprehension: *Falling Man*, part three

**Explain the meaning of the seven quotations from the third part of DeLillo's novel by re-reading and examining their contexts.**

1) Her mother, this is what she missed. (p. 184, l. 18)

2) Keith stared into the waterfall, forty yards away. (p. 195, l. 21)

3) "You want to kill somebody." (p. 204, l. 12)

4) He was a falling angel and his beauty was horrific. (p. 211, ll. 30–31)

5) There were nine people at mass today. (p. 225, l. 25)

6) He didn't know how he'd been cut. (p. 228, l. 8)

7) The briefcase came down and around the stairwell. (p. 234, l. 31)

Diese Impulsfrage, auf die zumindest kurze Antworten (etwa in Form eines Hinweises darauf, dass es sich um einen in New York nach den Anschlägen agierenden *performance artist* handelt) erwartet werden, leitet über zu einer arbeitsteiligen Partnerarbeit, in deren Verlauf die auf dem folgenden Arbeitsblatt (***Copy 18***) verzeichnete Tabelle auszufüllen ist.

What do we get to know about David Janiak and Lianne's reaction to him?

**Lösungsvorschläge zu *Copy 18*:**

**David Janiak:**

- a performance artist who brings back the moments in the WTC when people jumped from the windows
- always wears a safety harness, is assisted by his brother Roman
- appears unexpectedly among crowds
- studied acting and dramaturgy in Cambridge, Massachusetts, and in Moscow
- suffers from chronic depression and a heart ailment; dies at the age of 39 of natural causes
- was arrested several times for criminal trespasses
- performed his art in several places in New York City (e.g. Central Park, Carnegie Hall, a church in the Bronx, Queensboro Bridge)
- is believed to have imitated one of the 'jumpers' from the WTC, whose photo became known under the title of "Falling Man"

**Lianne's reaction to Falling Man:**

- she witnesses two of Janiak's performances in New York City (at Central Station and in the vicinity of a school)
- he reminds Lianne of the friends Keith has lost
- Lianne is fascinated by his art
- when she comes across his obituary in a newspaper, she starts to look for more information on the Internet
- he reminds her of a tarot card

**Janiak's function in the novel:**

- his performance art is closely related to the title of the novel and to one of its central topics: to bring back the memories of those people who jumped from the WTC, and, more generally, of all the victims of the terrorist attacks, including those who survived but continue to suffer from their traumatic experiences (like Keith)

Um die über David Janiak gewonnenen Erkenntnisse noch weiter zu vertiefen, erhalten die Schülerinnen und Schüler die Hausaufgabe, die Funktion dieser Figur für den gesamten Roman selbstständig zu bestimmen und ihre Überlegungen auf dem unteren Abschnitt des Arbeitsblattes zu notieren.

Describe Janiak's function in the novel and note down your ideas on the worksheet.

# David Janiak – Falling Man

**Re-read the following passages and fill in the grid:**

- Part one, chapter 4: p. 34, l. 6 – p. 35, l. 30
- Part two, chapter 9: p. 156, l. 13 – p. 158, l. 30; p. 160, l. 25 – p. 161, l. 29
- Part three, chapter 13: p. 208, l. 20 – p. 213, l. 29

| David Janiak (general information) | Lianne's reaction to Falling Man |
|---|---|
| | |

David Janiak's function in the novel:

Da die Behandlung des dritten Teils von *Falling Man* bislang primär eher traditionell analytisch ausgerichtet gewesen ist, liegt es aus didaktischen Gründen nahe, im Anschluss an die oben dargestellte Sequenz wenigstens punktuell einen methodisch alternativen Zugang zum Text vorzunehmen. Zwei Verfahren, ein produktions- und ein handlungsorientiertes, stehen hier zur Auswahl, von denen zumindest eines im Unterricht erprobt werden kann.
Den Ausgangspunkt des ersten, produktionsorientierten Verfahrens, das für eine Einzelstunde geeignet ist, bildet ein Zitat aus dem dritten Teil des Romans, auf das die Schülerinnen und Schüler bei der Bearbeitung des letzten *Worksheets* (vgl. ***Copy 18***) bereits gestoßen sein müssten. Da Lianne während ihrer Internetrecherche zu dem "Falling Man" genannten Künstler Janiak dessen spektakuläre Aktionen mit der bildlichen Vorstellung einer Tarotkarte assoziiert, lässt sich die entsprechende Textpassage gut zu Beginn der Stunde auf Folie präsentieren bzw. an die Tafel schreiben und mit der Aufgabe verbinden, diese Karte auf der Grundlage von Liannes Gedanken zeichnerisch zu entwerfen.

"She thought it could be the name of a trump card in a tarot deck, Falling Man, name in gothic type, the figure twisting down in a stormy night sky." (p. 211, ll. 5–7)

Draw a picture of the tarot card. What could it stand for?

Die Präsentation der Ergebnisse kann in verschiedener Weise erfolgen, beispielsweise in Form eines Museumsganges oder dadurch, dass die Zeichnungen kontinuierlich an den jeweils nächsten Sitznachbarn im Uhrzeigersinn weitergereicht werden, bis schließlich alle Schülerinnen und Schüler sämtliche Zeichnungen gesehen haben.
Die Beantwortung der Frage findet im anschließenden Unterrichtsgespräch statt, in dem der Lehrer/die Lehrerin darauf hinweist, dass es tatsächlich zwei Tarotkarten gibt, auf die DeLillos Roman in der oben zitierten Passage indirekt, aber dennoch deutlich Bezug nimmt: „The Tower", die erste der beiden auf ***Copy 19*** abgebildeten Karten, ist unter anderem von Verschwörungstheoretikern mit dem 11. September in Verbindung gebracht worden. Sie gilt als böses Omen und steht für Scheitern, Ruin und Katastrophen, aber auch für Veränderung im Allgemeinen. Einigen Deutungen zufolge bebildert sie die biblische Geschichte vom Turmbau zu Babel, in der Gott die Menschen für ihre Hybris bestraft und die babylonische Sprachverwirrung stiftet.
„The Hanged Man" hingegen stellt eine ambivalente Karte dar, die auch umgedreht betrachtet werden kann. Sie ist mit Opfer- und christlichen Erlösungsvorstellungen konnotiert und erinnert an den aus Liannes Perspektive beschriebenen ‚Schwebezustand' Janiaks am Ende seines Sprungs: "The jolting end of the fall left him upside-down, secured to the harness, twenty feet above the pavement [...] arms at his sides, one leg bent at the knee" (p. 161, ll. 18–22).
Die auf der Folie (***Copy 19***) abgebildeten Tarotkarten bieten Anlass zu einem abschließenden Unterrichtsgespräch, in dem die Schülerinnen und Schüler die Karten beschreiben, kommentieren und mit dem Roman in Beziehung setzen sollen.

What do the tarot cards show? How do you think they are related to the novel?

Die Hausaufgabe aus der Stunde, die dem Anforderungsbereich III (*Comment*) entspricht, erfüllt gleich zwei Funktionen: in Zusammenhang mit der Besprechung der Figur David Janiak bildet sie einen möglichen Schlusspunkt, zugleich weist sie auf die folgende Unterrichtssequenz zum Thema *Memory/Remembrance* (***Component 4***) voraus.

## *Falling Man* and tarot

Comment on David Janiak's artistic performances as an attempt to remind the public of 9/11.

Als Ausgangspunkt des zweiten, handlungsorientierten Verfahrens, für das eine Doppelstunde anzusetzen ist, fungiert ebenfalls ein Zitat aus dem dritten Teil des Romans, das aus dem Kontext der Internetrecherche von Lianne zu David Janiak stammt:

"She [Lianne] clicked forward to the transcript of a panel discussion at the New School. Falling Man as Heartless Exhibitionist or Brave New Chronicler of the Age of Terror." (part three, chapter 13, p. 210, ll. 1–3)

Die Schülerinnen und Schüler sind im Folgenden aufgefordert, eine Podiumsdiskussion mit verschiedenen Rollen zu eben dieser Kontroverse selbstständig vorzubereiten und durchzuführen. Nachdem die insgesamt sechs Rollen (***Copy 20***) per Zufallsprinzip verteilt worden sind (Mehrfachbesetzungen sind möglich), geht es darum, Kleingruppen zu bilden, deren Aufgabe darin besteht, Argumente aus der Perspektive der jeweiligen Figur zu entwickeln:

Against the background of this quotation from the novel, collect arguments for and/or against David Janiak's performances as Falling Man from your role character's point of view and prepare a contribution for a panel discussion in class.

Welches Gruppenmitglied in der anschließenden Podiumsdiskussion die Rolle tatsächlich übernimmt, bestimmen die Schülerinnen und Schüler selbst.
Nach der Diskussion besteht die Option, dass die Schülerinnen und Schüler sich begründet dazu äußern, welche Argumente am meisten überzeugt haben und welche Rolle am besten und glaubhaftesten verkörpert worden ist.
Die Hausaufgabe aus der Stunde geht aus der Podiumsdiskussion unmittelbar hervor, weist aber zugleich auf das noch folgende Thema *Memory/Remembrance* (**Component 4**) voraus.

Do you think that David Janiak's performances are an adequate means of reminding the public of the terrorist attacks of 9/11? Use at least three pros and three cons from the panel discussion.

## 3.4 The 'real' Falling Man

Der folgende Textausschnitt aus dem in der ursprünglichen Fassung wesentlich längeren Artikel „The Falling Man" (***Copy 21***) ist 2003 in der Zeitschrift *Esquire* erschienen und hat für großes Aufsehen gesorgt, da sein Autor, der Journalist Tom Junod, darin den Versuch unternimmt, die Identität des „Falling Man" auf dem berühmten Foto von Richard Drew vom 11. September zu klären. Drew war bereits zuvor als Fotograf des Kennedy-Attentats in die Geschichte eingegangen. Sein Foto vom 11. September erschien am Tag nach den Anschlägen auf Seite 7 der *New York Times* und löste einen Sturm des Protestes aus, weshalb es anschließend lange nicht mehr gedruckt wurde.
Das zu Beginn der gesamten Unterrichtsreihe gezeigte Foto vom ‚wirklichen' „Falling Man" (vgl. ***Getting Started***) wird nun erneut auf den Tageslichtprojektor gelegt, um zum einen nach der Besprechung der Hausaufgabe einen Konnex zu David Janiak herzustellen und zum anderen zu Junods Artikel hinzuführen. Die Leitfrage für die Lektüre und Erschließung des Textausschnitts in Partnerarbeit lautet:

# Role cards for a panel discussion

Role: liberal arts student

You come from Munich, Germany, where you are a member of a drama group at the university.

You read about David Janiak on the Internet and are fascinated by his performances.

You are an advocate of artistic freedom.

Role: Rumsey's mother

You lost your only son in the north tower of the World Trade Center.

Since the loss is still very painful for you, you do not want to be reminded of his death.

Role: Egyptian owner of a grocery store close to Ground Zero

You watched the towers collapse.

You are undecided what to think about Falling Man.

You feel deeply sorry for the victims of the terrorist attacks and you insist on the fact that most Muslims are moderate.

Role: Roman Janiak

You are a software engineer and assisted your brother David with most performances.

Although you were always worried about your brother's safety, you have been his biggest fan.

Now you are looking for someone to follow in your brother's artistic footsteps.

Role: New York policeman

You arrested David Janiak after one of his performances for "criminal trespass, reckless endangerment and disorderly conduct" (part three, chapter 13, p. 209, ll. 30–31).

You are strictly against any kind of unauthorized private performances in public and you prefer official commemorations instead.

Role: leader of the discussion

Your job is to ask questions which keep the discussion going.

Try to mediate between opposing positions.

Do not forget to ask the audience to pose further questions and to make comments at the end of the discussion.

What does the text tell you about the 'real' Falling Man? Take notes.

**Lösungsvorschläge zu *Copy 21*:**

- moral dilemma: the author's curiosity vs the hurt feelings of the bereaved
- Junod identifies the Falling Man as Jonathan Briley, who worked at the restaurant on top of the north tower
- Briley was a light-skinned black man, 43 years old, tall, wore a beard and has short hair
- his wife's name is Hillary and his father is a preacher
- he has a brother and a sister; his brother Timothy keeps one of his shoes as a memorial
- his sister thinks that her brother decided to jump because he suffered from asthma
- but: there is no final certainty about the identity of the Falling Man
- according to the author, the photo serves as a kind of memorial to posterity (l. 54: "The picture is his cenotaph")

# Tom Junod, "The Falling Man"

Do you remember this photograph? In the United States, people have taken pains to banish it from the record of September 11, 2001. The story behind it, though, and the search for the man pictured in it, are our most intimate connection to the horror of that day. [...]
Of course, the only way to find out the identity of the Falling Man is to call the families of anyone who might be the Falling Man and ask what they know about their son's or husband's or father's last day on earth. Ask if he went to work wearing an orange shirt.
But should those calls be made? Should those questions be asked? Would they only heap pain upon the already anguished? Would they be regarded as an insult to the memory of the dead, the way the Hernandez family regarded the imputation[1] that Norberto Hernandez[2] was the Falling Man? Or would they be regarded as steps to some act of redemptive[3] witness?
Jonathan Briley worked at Windows on the World. Some of his co-workers, when they saw Richard Drew's photographs, thought he might be the Falling Man. He was a light-skinned black man. He was over six five[4]. He was forty-three. He had a mustache and a goatee[5] and close-cropped hair. He had a wife named Hillary.
Jonathan Briley's father is a preacher, a man who has devoted his whole life to serving the Lord. After September 11, he gathered his family together to ask God to tell him where his son was. No: he demanded it. He used these words: "Lord, I demand to know where my son is." For three hours straight, he prayed in his deep voice, until he spent the grace he had accumulated over a lifetime in the insistence of his appeal.
The next day, the FBI called. They'd found his son's body. It was, miraculously, intact.
The preacher's youngest son, Timothy, went to identify his brother. He recognized him by his shoes: he was wearing black high-tops. Timothy removed one of them and took it home and put it in his garage, as a kind of memorial.
Timothy knew all about the Falling Man. He is a cop in Mount Vernon, New York, and in the week after his brother died, someone had left a September 12 newspaper open in the locker room. He saw the photograph of the Falling Man and, in anger, he refused to look at it again. But he couldn't throw it away. Instead, he stuffed it in the bottom of his locker, where – like the black shoe in his garage – it became permanent.
Jonathan's sister Gwendolyn knew about the Falling Man, too. She saw the picture the day it was published. She knew that Jonathan had asthma, and in the smoke and the heat would have done anything just to breathe ...
The both of them, Timothy and Gwendolyn, knew what Jonathan wore to work on most days. He wore a white shirt and black pants, along with the high-top black shoes. Timothy also knew what Jonathan sometimes wore under his shirt: an orange T-shirt. Jonathan wore that orange T-shirt everywhere. He wore that shirt all the time. He wore it so often that Timothy used to make fun of him: When are you gonna get rid of that orange T-shirt, Slim?
But when Timothy identified his brother's body, none of his clothes were recognizable except the black shoes. And when Jonathan went to work on the morning of September 11, 2001, he'd left early and kissed his wife goodbye while she was still sleeping. She never saw the clothes he was wearing. After she learned that he was dead, she packed his clothes away and never inventoried what specific articles of clothing might be missing.
Is Jonathan Briley the Falling Man? He might be. But maybe he didn't jump from the window as a betrayal of love or because he lost hope. Maybe he jumped to fulfill the terms of a miracle. Maybe he jumped to come home to his family. Maybe he didn't jump at all, because no one can jump into the arms of God.
Oh, no. You have to fall.

Yes, Jonathan Briley might be the Falling Man. But the only certainty we have is the certainty we had at the start: at fifteen seconds after 9:41 a.m., on September 11, 2001, a photographer named Richard Drew took a picture of a man falling through the sky – falling through time as well as through space. The picture went all around the world, and then disappeared, as if we willed it away. One of the most famous photographs in human history became an unmarked grave, and the man buried inside its frame – the Falling Man – became the Unknown Soldier in a war whose end we have not yet seen. Richard Drew's photograph is all we know of him, and yet all we know of him becomes a measure of what we know of ourselves. The picture is his cenotaph[6], and like the monuments dedicated to the memory of unknown soldiers everywhere, it asks that we look at it, and make one simple acknowledgment.

That we have known who the Falling Man is all along.

from: *Esquire* 140, no 3 (September 2003), 177–178, http://www.esquire.com/features/articles/2003/030903_mfe_falling_1.html [20.8.11]

[1] **imputation** being charged with a crime or fault, accusation; [2] **Norberto Hernandez** A pastry chef who worked in the restaurant at the top of the World Trade Center (Windows on the World); he was the first out of three men who were thought to be the 'real' Falling Man; [3] **redemptive** delivering a soul from sin and damnation; [4] **over six five** over six feet and five inches (about 1.95 metres); [5] **goatee** a beard trimmed in the form of a tuft hanging from the chin, resembling that of a he-goat; [6] **cenotaph** an empty tomb; a sepulchral monument erected in honour of a deceased person whose body is elsewhere

Component 4

# Losing memory and acts of remembrance

Das Thema der Erinnerung ist für den Roman insgesamt strukturbildend. Im Rahmen dieser Unterrichtssequenz geht es darum, die für den Text zentrale Dichotomie von Erinnerung und Vergessen wie auch den Zusammenhang von individueller und kollektiver Erinnerung herauszuarbeiten, ohne dabei auf voraussetzungsreiche theoretische Konzepte zurückgreifen zu müssen.

## 4.1 Approaching the topic of memory

Ungeachtet der Tatsache, dass mit dem Thema der Erinnerung in *Falling Man* durchweg sehr ernsthafte Aspekte verknüpft sind, steht ein eher spielerischer Einstieg in Form eines Gedächtnistests (***Copy 22***), der zugleich auch der Wiederholung zentraler Begriffe des Romans dient, am Beginn dieser Unterrichtssequenz. Die Folie wird für 60 Sekunden auf den Tageslichtschreiber gelegt, innerhalb derer sich die Schülerinnen und Schüler die Stichworte in der richtigen Reihenfolge einzuprägen versuchen.
Die im Anschluss unternommenen Versuche, die Begriffe auswendig vor der Gruppe zu rekapitulieren, werden vermutlich zu der Einsicht führen, dass die Merkfähigkeit des menschlichen Gehirns begrenzt ist. Deshalb lässt der Kursleiter/die Kursleiterin die Schülerinnen und Schüler darüber nachdenken, warum ausgerechnet diese Aufgabe am Anfang der Stunde steht:

> Why do you think we did a memory test like this?

Diese Frage leitet über zur Rolle des Themenkomplexes *Memory/Remembrance* in DeLillos *Falling Man*. Um das Vorwissen der Schülerinnen und Schüler zu ermitteln, erfolgt zunächst ein Brainstorming:

> What do you associate with memory? Take notes.

Bei der Sammlung der Ergebnisse an der Tafel fordert der Lehrer/die Lehrerin dazu auf, zwischen individuellem und kollektivem Gedächtnis zu unterscheiden:

# Test your memory

Have a look at the list of words for one minute and try to remember them in the correct order.

Morandi still lives

planes

briefcase

poker

monosyllables

Falling Man

memory

music

jihadists

organic shrapnel

| Memory | |
|---|---|
| individual | collective |
| personal experience | history |
| families and friends | fairy tales, novels |
| love, relationships | culture in general |
| thoughts and beliefs | language |
| souvenirs | media |
| personal habits | religion, rites |
| birthdays, anniversaries | memorial days |
| ↓ | ↓ |
| transient, 'dies' with the person/generation | permanent, transmitted to the next generation |

Nach der Sammlung der Ergebnisse ist die nahe liegende Frage zu stellen, welche der an der Tafel notierten Aspekte für den Roman von Bedeutung sind. Diese können dann an der Tafel unterstrichen werden.

Which of these aspects are relevant for the novel?

Eine Erkenntnis, zu der die Schülerinnen und Schüler im Verlauf des Unterrichtsgesprächs vermutlich gelangen werden, besteht darin, dass viele der von ihnen genannten Aspekte in *Falling Man* auszumachen sind (und sich dabei teilweise überlappen). Dementsprechend stellt sich DeLillos Roman hinsichtlich seiner grundlegenden Thematik der Terroranschläge vom 11. September 2001 als eine Art Schnittstelle von individueller und kollektiver Erinnerungspraxis dar.

## 4.2 Losing memory: Alzheimer's disease in *Falling Man*

In DeLillos Roman ist die Thematik der Erinnerung auf das Engste verknüpft mit der des Vergessens, wie sich am Beispiel der von Lianne Glenn ehrenamtlich betreuten Gruppe von Alzheimerpatienten aufzeigen lässt. Um zum Motiv des Vergessens überzuleiten, kann folgende Frage an den Kurs gerichtet werden:

What does a loss of memory mean/imply?

Die vermutlich zunächst eher allgemein gehaltenen Antworten (Orientierungslosigkeit, Sprach- und Identitätsverlust etc.) gilt es mit Blick auf die für den Roman zentrale Alzheimererkrankung zu konkretisieren:

What do you know about Alzheimer's disease?

Diese Frage kann durchaus auch zum Anlass genommen werden, persönliche Erfahrungen im Umgang mit Menschen, die an Alzheimer oder Demenz erkrankt sind, zu thematisieren. Zur Versachlichung des Themas trägt das Informationsblatt bei (***Copy 23***), das auf einem im Internet frei zugänglichen Symptomkatalog der amerkanischen *Alzheimer's Association* beruht.
Nach der gemeinsamen Lektüre des Blattes richtet sich die Aufmerksamkeit wieder auf DeLillos Roman:

## Where does the topic of dementia/Alzheimer's disease appear in the novel?

Damit die Schülerinnen und Schüler Liannes Alzheimergruppe genauer in den Blick nehmen können, schreibt der Lehrer/die Lehrerin Angaben zu ausgewählten Romanstellen an die Tafel und verteilt ein Arbeitsblatt (***Copy 24***). Auf der Grundlage einer erneuten Lektüre dieser Passagen soll das Arbeitsblatt anschließend in Partnerarbeit ausgefüllt werden, wobei die Option eines arbeitsteiligen Vorgehens gegeben ist (mögliche Aufteilung: a) Lianne und b) Mitglieder).

**Re-read the following passages about Lianne's Alzheimer group:**

| | |
|---|---|
| Part one: | chapter 4: p. 31, l. 1 – p. 33, l. 14 |
| | chapter 5: p. 61, ll. 9–29 |
| Part two: | chapter 6: p. 93, l. 4 – p. 95, l. 5 |
| | chapter 7: p. 123, ll. 1–30 |
| Part three: | chapter 10: p. 181, l. 5 – p. 182, l. 3 |

### Lösungsvorschläge zu *Copy 24:*

| conductor | personal background/motivation |
|---|---|
| Lianne Glenn | • group was started by a clinical psychologist and taken over by Lianne about two years before the terrorist attacks<br>• she is warned by Dr Apter not to increase the frequency of the meetings to twice a week out of egoistic motives<br>→ therapeutic function of the sessions for herself against the background of her father's diagnosed dementia and suicide<br>• she believes herself to suffer from memory lapses and takes tests and medical examination<br>→ she is afraid of having the same genetic disposition for dementia as her father ("bearing her father's mark" [p. 123, l. 8]) |

| member | general information | pathological symptoms |
|---|---|---|
| Rosellen S. | • small woman of delicate features, dark-skinned<br>• likes to write about childhood memories<br>• when she was 10 years old, her father came home after 4 years of disappearance<br>• her sister lives in Brooklyn | • one day she suddenly cannot remember where she lives<br>• loses sense of clarity |
| Omar H. | • he is the only one who lives in a different area of NYC (lower East side)<br>• compares the meetings to prayers<br>• is nervous at the thought of writing about 9/11 | • has problems to organize his weekly trips by subway to the sessions |
| Carmen G. | • likes to insert Spanish expressions into her writings<br>• is interested in Benny T. | • has language problems<br>• fast decline of her intellectual capacities<br>• gets confused with time |

# Some facts about Alzheimer's disease

## 10 warning signs of Alzheimer's disease

1 Memory loss that disrupts daily life
2 Challenges in planning or solving problems
3 Difficulty completing familiar tasks at home, at work or at leisure
4 Confusion with time or space
5 Trouble understanding visual images and spatial relationships
6 New problems with words in speaking or writing
7 Misplacing things and losing the ability to retrace steps
8 Decreased or poor judgment
9 Withdrawal from work or social activities
10 Changes in mood and personality

## The difference between Alzheimer's and typical age-related changes

| Signs of Alzheimer's | Typical age-related changes |
|---|---|
| Poor judgment and decision making | Making a bad decision once in a while |
| Inability to manage a budget | Missing a monthly payment |
| Losing track of the date or the season | Forgetting which day it is and remembering later |
| Difficulty having a conversation | Sometimes forgetting which word to use |
| Misplacing things and being unable to retrace steps to find them | Losing things from time to time |

quoted from: Alzheimer's association, www.alz.org/alzheimers_disease_10_signs_of_alzheimers.asp

# Losing memory: Lianne's storyline sessions

What do you get to know about
a) Lianne and her motivation to conduct the Alzheimer group?
b) the different members of the group and the symptoms they show?
Fill in the grid.

| **conductor** | **personal background/motivation** |
|---|---|
| Lianne Glenn | |

| **member** | **general information** | **pathological symptoms** |
|---|---|---|
| Rosellen S. | | |
| Omar H. | | |
| Carmen G. | | |
| Benny T. | | |
| Anna C. | | |
| Curtis B. | | |

| member | general information | pathological symptoms |
|---|---|---|
| Benny T. | • hates writing and loves talking<br>• is considered good-looking by Carmen G.<br>• was not married<br>• brings pastry to the group meetings which nobody eats | • has problems putting his pants on<br>• feels that he is not in his own mind and body |
| Anna C. | • broad-bodied<br>• writes about the revelation of writing | |
| Curtis B. | • 81 years old<br>• tall and taciturn<br>• has read the whole *Encyclopedia Britannica*<br>• was imprisoned for having killed a man with a broken bottle in a bar fight | • often loses things<br>• cannot put his watch on his wrist |

Beim Zusammentragen und Vergleich der Ergebnisse im Kursverbund, beispielsweise auf einer Folie, ergibt sich für die Schülerinnen und Schüler ein klareres Bild der einzelnen Mitglieder der Selbsthilfegruppe sowie der persönlichen Motive, die Lianne zur Anleitung der Gruppe veranlassen. Darüber hinaus finden sich auf dem Arbeitsblatt eine Reihe exakt jener pathologischen Symptome wieder, die sich unschwer mit den von der amerikanischen Alzheimergesellschaft aufgelisteten Warnzeichen (***Copy 23***) in Verbindung bringen lassen:

To which of the "10 warning signs of Alzheimer's disease" do the pathological symptoms of Lianne's patients correspond?

Sofern es die verbleibende Unterrichtszeit dieser ohnehin inhaltlich gut ausgefüllten Doppelstunde erlaubt, können die entsprechenden Warnzeichen in Form von Ziffern in Klammern hinter die auf dem Arbeitsblatt (***Copy 24***) aufgelisteten Symptome notiert werden. So trifft etwa, um nur ein Beispiel zu nennen, auf Rosellens Krankheitsbild (one day she suddenly cannot remember where she lives) der vierte der zehn Aspekte zu (confusion with time or space).
Die folgende Hausaufgabe stellt zum einen eine Verbindung zwischen individueller und kollektiver Erinnerung her und führt zum anderen zu der abschließend zu diskutierenden Frage, welchen Beitrag DeLillos Roman zum kollektiven Gedächtnis zu leisten vermag.

How would you remind the public of 9/11? Develop and note down some ideas.

## 4.3 Acts of remembrance

Noch vor der Besprechung der Hausaufgabe ist eine Folie mit Fotos von *Ground Zero* und dem Holocaust Denkmal in Berlin aufzulegen (***Copy 25***). Da die Bilder selbst einen hohen Wiedererkennungswert haben und genug Gesprächsanlass bieten, kann zunächst auf einen verbalen Impuls verzichtet werden. Um das Unterrichtsgespräch in Gang zu halten, kann auf folgende Fragen zurückgegriffen werden:

Has anybody ever been to these places? What do you think of the Holocaust Memorial in Berlin and/or of memorials in general?

Dass sich einzelne Schülerinnen und Schüler in ihrer Hausaufgabe für ein Denkmal als Medium der kollektiven Erinnerung entschieden haben werden, ist sehr wahrscheinlich. Deshalb schließt sich eine ausführliche Besprechung der zu Hause entwickelten Ideen an. Hierbei besteht die Option, die genannten Vorschläge unkommentiert von einzelnen Schülerinnen und Schülern an der Tafel zu notieren, um auf diese Weise gemeinsam einen Katalog potenzieller Erinnerungsmedien und -mittel zu erstellen. Unabhängig davon, ob in diesem Zusammenhang literarisches Schreiben (auch von Gedichten oder Songs) als Erinnerungspraxis bereits in den Blick kommt, ist DeLillos Roman unbedingt namentlich in die Diskussion einzubringen, etwa mithilfe der folgenden Fragen:

> What about *Falling Man* in this context? Would you consider DeLillo's novel as an act of remembrance as well?

Um den Roman insgesamt noch einmal daraufhin zu untersuchen, ob und inwiefern DeLillo mit *Falling Man* einen Beitrag zum Gedenken an 9/11 geliefert hat, sind die Kursteilnehmerinnen und -teilnehmer aufgefordert, konkret entsprechende inhaltliche wie auch strukturelle Aspekte zu ermitteln:

> How does *Falling Man* contribute to the remembrance of 9/11? Consider both the novel's content and structure and take notes.

Die Bearbeitung dieser Aufgabe könnte zu folgendem Tafelbild als Ergebnis führen:

**Writing to remember: *Falling Man* as an act of remembrance**

1) content:
- example of the Neudecker family: physical and psychological consequences
- the story of Florence Givens as another example
- attempt to explore the mind of a terrorist (Hammad)
- portrait of an artist reminding the public (David Janiak)

2) structure:
- cyclical structure (last chapter of the book narrates the very moment of the attack and chronologically takes place before the first one)
- fragmented narration: the novel itself is 'in pieces'

Um am Ende der Unterrichtsreihe von der komplexen und abstrakten analytischen Ebene zur persönlichen Leseerfahrung der Schülerinnen und Schüler zurückzukehren, gilt es noch im Unterrichtsgespräch folgende Frage zu klären:

> Which aspects do you personally think are worth remembering about DeLillo's *Falling Man*?

## 4.4 Evaluating *Falling Man*

Abschließend erhalten die Kursteilnehmerinnen und -teilnehmer einen Evaluationsbogen (***Copy 26***), den sie entweder während der Stunde oder zu Hause ausfüllen. Die Evaluation erfüllt den doppelten Zweck, dass aufgrund der Anonymität des Verfahrens die Möglichkeit einer freien Meinungsäußerung gegeben ist und dass eine Auswertung Aufschluss darüber gibt, ob der Roman wie auch dessen Behandlung im Unterricht das Interesse der Schülerinnen und Schüler zu wecken vermochten. Bei zwei unterschiedlichen Lerngruppen hat dies etwa zu dem Ergebnis geführt, dass der Text selbst aufgrund seines hohen Komplexitätsgrades und seines Sprachniveaus zwar auf wenig Gegenliebe gestoßen, aber in thematischer Hinsicht von einer breiten Mehrheit als durchaus interessant und aktuell eingestuft worden ist.

# *Falling Man* in class – an evaluation

**1) Do you think that *Falling Man* is worth reading?**

Yes ☐ No ☐ Undecided ☐

**2) Describe your personal impressions of the novel.**

______________________________

______________________________

**3) Did the novel fulfil your expectations?**

Yes ☐ No ☐ Undecided ☐

Explain why or why not:

______________________________

______________________________

**4) On a scale from one to ten, how difficult do you consider the novel?**

______________________________

What I consider most difficult:

______________________________

**5) On a scale from one to ten, how interesting do you find its topic (9/11)?**

______________________________

What I consider most interesting:

______________________________

**6) Do you think that *Falling Man* is an appropriate novel for an English elementary course (Grund-kurs)?**

Yes ☐ No ☐ Undecided ☐

Explain why or why not:

______________________________

______________________________

**7) My suggestions for improving classroom discussion of *Falling Man*:**

______________________________

______________________________

Component 5

# Songs about 9/11

Diese *Component* ist weder als eigenständige noch ausdrücklich als chronologisch letzte Unterrichtssequenz angelegt, sondern vielmehr als Angebot aufzufassen, auf das zu nahezu jedem Zeitpunkt im Verlauf der gesamten Reihe zurückgegriffen werden kann. Erfahrungsgemäß ist es sinnvoll, eines der oder beide Lieder im Anschluss an die Klausur zu behandeln, um nach einer intensiven analytischen Auseinandersetzung mit dem komplexen Roman einen eher affektiven Zugang zur Thematik zu ermöglichen.
In den inzwischen zirka zehn Jahren, die seit den Anschlägen auf das World Trade Center vergangen sind, haben sich eine Vielzahl von Musikern und Bands weltweit mit dieser Thematik befasst. In diesem Zusammenhang ist die von Jeffrey Melnick verfasste Monographie *9/11 Culture: America under Construction* (Malden, Massachusetts: Wiley-Blackwell, 2009) zu empfehlen, die im Anhang eine fünfseitige Auflistung von auf diese Thematik bezogenen Liedern und Alben enthält (a.a.O., S. 172–76). Vollständig ist diese Liste keineswegs; so fehlt etwa nicht nur der Titel „Sacrificed Sons" von *Dream Theater* (vgl. 5.2), sondern auch der äußerst umstrittene, ebenso provokante wie plakative Song „Jihad" der amerikanischen Thrash-Metal Band *Slayer* aus dem Jahr 2009.

## 5.1 Bruce Springsteen, "Into the Fire" (2002)

Der international überaus erfolgreiche amerikanische Rockmusiker Bruce Springsteen (Jahrgang 1949) veröffentlichte im Jahr 2002 gemeinsam mit der *E Street Band* das Album *The Rising*, das unter dem Eindruck der Terroranschläge vom 11. September und Berichten zufolge auf speziellen Wunsch seiner Fans entstanden ist. Im Kontext der Reihe zu *Falling Man* bietet sich der Einsatz von „Into the Fire" besonders an, weil Springsteen in diesem Lied ebenfalls, ähnlich wie DeLillo in seinem Roman, ein apokalyptisches Szenario von den brennenden Türmen entwirft. Im Unterschied zu den beiden im Roman dargestellten erfolgreichen Fluchtversuchen von Keith Neudecker und Florence Givens führt der Weg des von Springsteen besungenen Feuerwehrmanns nicht die Treppen des einsturzbedrohten Gebäudes hinab in die Freiheit, sondern, im Gegenteil, die Stufen hinauf, was seinen sicheren Tod bedeutet.
Eine mögliche *pre-listening activity* zu diesem Lied besteht darin, die Schülerinnen und Schüler anhand des Titels darüber spekulieren zu lassen, worum es in „Into the Fire" inhaltlich gehen könnte:

> Bruce Springsteen's song "Into the Fire" was composed as a reaction to the terrorist attacks of 9/11. What does the title tell you about its content?

Sollte kein Schülerbeitrag auf die Schicksale der in der medialen Öffentlichkeit vielfach glorifizierten Feuerwehrmänner verweisen, die DeLillo in seinem Roman ausspart, kann der Lehrer/die Lehrerin explizit auf die Bedeutung der Präposition „into" aufmerksam machen.

Beim erstmaligen Anhören des Liedes (ohne Textblatt) geht es darum, erste Eindrücke zu sammeln und ein Globalverständnis des Inhaltes zu sichern:

> Describe the song in terms of content and atmosphere.

Was schon beim ersten Hören auffällt, sind die positive Grundstimmung des Liedes, die im Kontrast zu den wahrscheinlichen Erwartungen der Schülerinnen und Schüler steht, und die Wiederholung der religiös aufgeladenen Schlüsselwörter *strength*, *faith*, *hope* und *love*, deren ebenso ermutigender wie beschwörender Charakter die düsteren Aspekte des Songs überdeckt.
Um zu einem genaueren Verständnis des Liedes zu gelangen, erhalten die Kursteilnehmerinnen und -teilnehmer nun das Textblatt (***Copy 27***) und folgende Hör- bzw. Arbeitsaufträge:

> Listen to the song again and answer the following questions by taking notes:
>
> **1.** What do you get to know about the firefighter and the situation he is in?
>
> **2.** Who is the speaker?
>
> **3.** What is the message of the song?

Nach dem Hören bekommen die Schülerinnen und Schüler nicht nur die Gelegenheit, die Bedeutung unbekannter Vokabeln zu erfragen, sondern auch genügend Zeit, ihre Notizen zu machen.
Die Ergebnissicherung erfolgt an der Tafel:

**Bruce Springsteen, "Into the Fire"**

1. firefighter: went up the stairs of one of the burning towers where he died (cf. l. 21: "smoky grave")
2. speaker: presumably his wife or girlfriend who misses her former partner but tries to find consolation in the thought that he fulfilled his duty for the love of God and his country
3. message: song as a kind of obituary for a firefighter who died on 9/11 in an act of heroic self-sacrifice (model function)

An die Besprechung des Liedes schließt sich noch eine in Partnerarbeit zu beantwortende Aufgabe an, bei der es um mögliche Gemeinsamkeiten und Unterschieden zwischen „Into the Fire" und *Falling Man* geht:

> Compare "Into the Fire" and *Falling Man* with each other and point out similarities and differences.
>
> **Lösungsvorschläge:**
>
> ***similarities:***
> - both the first chapter of the novel and the song describe an apocalyptic scenario (motifs: blood, dust, smoke)
> - the stairs of the north tower play an important role in *Falling Man*, too (flight situations, picking up the briefcase)

# Bruce Springsteen, "Into the Fire"

The sky was falling and streaked with blood
I heard you calling me, then you disappeared into dust
Up the stairs, into the fire/Up the stairs, into the fire
I need your kiss, but love and duty called you someplace higher
Somewhere up the stairs, into the fire

May your strength give us strength
May your faith give us faith
May your hope give us hope
May your love give us love (2 times)

You gave your love to see, in fields of red and autumn brown
You gave your love to me and lay your young body down
Up the stairs, into the fire/Up the stairs, into the fire
I need you near, but love and duty called you someplace higher
Somewhere up the stairs, into the fire

May your strength give us strength
May your faith give us faith
May your hope give us hope
May your love give us love (3 times)

It was dark, too dark to see, you held me
In the light you gave, you lay your hand on me
Then walked into the darkness of your smoky grave
Up the stairs, into the fire/Up the stairs, into the fire
I need your kiss, but love and duty called you someplace higher
Somewhere up the stairs, into the fire

May your strength give us strength
May your faith give us faith
May your hope give us hope
May your love bring us love (4 times)



**streaked** marked with streaks; striped

***differences:***

- none of DeLillo's main characters is a firefighter
- whereas Florence Givens and Keith Neudecker managed to escape from the burning north tower by going down the stairs, the firefighter in Springsteen's song climbed up the stairs and died in one of the towers
- DeLillo's novel is much more pessimistic than Springsteen's encouraging song
- *Falling Man* is not patriotic and presents no 'heroes' but rather 'ordinary' people seriously traumatized by the events

Was die Besprechung der Ergebnisse im Unterricht betrifft, erscheint in diesem Fall eine vollständige Sicherung an der Tafel nicht unbedingt erforderlich; lediglich der zuletzt genannte Aspekt könnte unterhalb des weiter oben skizzierten Tafelbildes (Bruce Springsteen, "Into the Fire") festgehalten werden, da er durchaus zu einem vertiefenden Verständnis von *Falling Man* beiträgt:

↔ *Falling Man* is not patriotic and presents no 'heroes' but rather 'ordinary' people seriously traumatized by the events

Falls das zweite Lied (*Dream Theater*, „Sacrificed Sons") nicht mehr innerhalb der Unterrichtsreihe zum Einsatz kommt, kann bereits an dieser Stelle die am Ende des folgenden Teilkapitels (5.2) formulierte Transferfrage, ob und inwieweit Rockmusik ein angemessenes Medium der Verarbeitung der Terroranschläge vom 11. September ist, an die Schülerinnen und Schüler gerichtet oder ihnen als Hausaufgabe gestellt werden.

## 5.2 *Dream Theater*, "Sacrificed Sons" (2005)

*Dream Theaters* Lied „Sacrificed Sons", das auf dem achten Studioalbum *Octavarium* (2005) der amerikanischen *Progressive Metal*-Band zu finden ist, erscheint für den Einsatz im Unterricht insofern besonders geeignet, als es mit einem knapp einminütigem Intro beginnt, das auch isoliert als Einstiegsimpuls zu Beginn einer Stunde dienen kann. In diesem Intro ist eine beklemmende Kakophonie von Stimmen in arabischer und englischer Sprache, vereinzelten Geigenklängen, zunehmend bedrohlicher werdenden Geräuschen und nicht zuletzt von authentischen Radio- und Fernsehkommentaren vom 11. September zu hören, unter ihnen Aussagen von George W. Bush, der eine erbarmungslose ‚Jagd' auf die verantwortlichen Terroristen ankündigt ("terrorism against our nation will not stand", "the government will hunt down those responsible"). Aufgrund seiner unmittelbaren emotionalen Wirkung auf den Hörer lässt sich dieses Intro unkommentiert als stummer Impuls einsetzen. Alternativ können folgende Höraufträge erteilt werden:

1. Describe what you hear.
2. What kind of atmosphere is created?

Das Intro kann auch mehrfach abgespielt werden, um ein genaues Hörverständnis der gesprochenen (Halb-)Sätze zu ermöglichen.

Nach diesem betont affektiven Einstieg informiert der Lehrer/die Lehrerin die Kursmitglieder über den Titel des Songs und fordert sie zugleich auf, ihre Assoziationen in einer Mindmap festzuhalten:

The song is called "Sacrificed Sons." What do you associate with this title? Note down your ideas in a mind map.

Ist im Klassenraum eine aufklappbare Tafel vorhanden, besteht die Option, zwei Schüler/innen auszuwählen, die ihre Mindmaps auf die Rückseiten der Tafel schreiben, sodass ein Vergleich beider Varianten möglich wird. Hier ein Lösungsvorschlag:

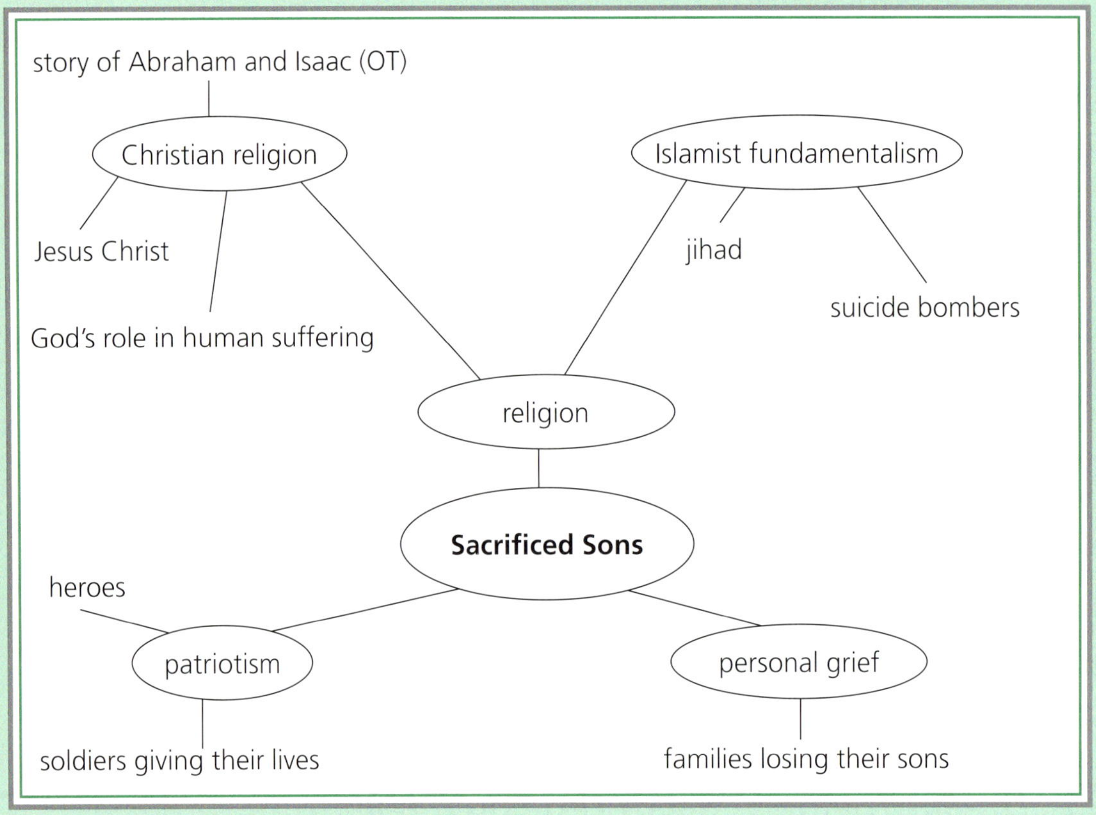


Nachdem die Schülerinnen und Schüler ihre Assoziation in Zusammenhang mit dem Titel vorgestellt, miteinander verglichen und diskutiert haben, erhalten sie das Textblatt (***Copy 28***) und hören das Lied zumindest ein Mal in voller Länge. Mit Blick auf die Unterrichtsplanung ist zu bedenken, dass der Song insgesamt mehr als 10 Minuten dauert und einen längeren Instrumentalteil enthält.
Im Anschluss daran gibt es zwei *post-listening activities*, die wahlweise in Partnerarbeit oder in Kleingruppen zu bearbeiten sind:

Work on the following tasks by taking notes:

1. Who are the "Sacrificed Sons"?
2. Try to divide the song into different parts and describe what they are about.

**Lösungsvorschläge**:

1. The chorus line "All praise their Sacrificed sons" is ambiguous/has a double meaning: first and foremost, it refers to the suicide bombers, who sacrificed their lives for a seemingly higher cause (jihad); second, in connection with the line "Heroes die" (l. 16), it may also allude to the victims of the attacks (including the firefighters, who lost their lives in the towers)

**2.** Three different parts: the first part (ll. 1–16) presents the events of 9/11 and people's reactions to them as they were shown on different TV channels (l. 3: "Channel surfing"); the second part is the chorus (ll. 17–23; 32–38), which reflects on the fundamentalist religious motivation of the terrorists (ll. 21, 36: "Scriptures they heed have misled them"); the third part (ll. 24–31; 39–44) criticizes the fundamentalists who preach hatred instead of the love of God and poses the question whether mankind is to blame for its mistakes; the last line, in which the speaker appeals to God for help, is a pun on the common curse "For Heaven's sake" (l. 44)

Da die *Lyrics* sehr suggestiv sind, ist davon auszugehen, dass die von den Schülerinnen und Schülern erarbeiteten Ergebnisse sehr unterschiedlich ausfallen werden. Eine ausführliche mündliche Präsentation mit anschließender Diskussion ist deshalb unbedingt einzuplanen. An die Besprechung des Liedes kann sich die folgende Transferfrage anschließen, die alternativ auch als Hausaufgabe zu stellen ist:

Do you think that rock songs like Bruce Springsteen's "Into the Fire" and/or *Dream Theater's* "Sacrificed Sons" are suitable means to deal with the topic of 9/11? Give reasons for your opinion.

# *Dream Theater, "Sacrificed Sons"*

Walls are closing
Anxiously
Channel surfing[1]
Frantically[2]

Burning City
Smoke and fire
Planes we're certain
Faith inspired

No clues
A complete surprise
Who'll be
Coming home tonight

Heads all turning
Towards the sky
Towers crumble
Heroes die

Who would wish this on
On our people
And proclaim
That His will be done
Scriptures they heed[3] have misled them
All praise their Sacrificed sons
All praise their Sacrificed sons

*Instrumental Part*

Teach them
What to think and feel
Your ways
So enlightening

Words they preach
I can't relate
If God's true Love
Are acts of Hate

Who would wish this on
On our people
And proclaim
That His will be done
Scriptures they heed have misled them
All praise their Sacrificed sons
All praise their Sacrificed sons

God on High
Our mistake
Will mankind be extinct?
There's no time to waste
Who serves the truth
For Heaven's sake



[1] **channel surfing** the practice of changing frequently between television channels
[2] **frantically** madly
[3] **heed** give attention to, regard

# Weiterführende Materialien

## 1. Texte von Don DeLillo aus dem Kontext von *Falling Man*


- "In the Ruins of the Future: Reflections on Terror and Loss in the Shadow of September," *Harper's Magazine*, December 2001, 33–40.
- "Baader-Meinhof," *The New Yorker*, 1 April 2002, 78–82.
- *Cosmopolis*. New York: Scribner, 2003.


## 2. Literaturhinweise zu *Falling Man* und 9/11


- Duvall, John N., ed., *The Cambridge Companion to Don DeLillo* (Cambridge: Cambridge University Press, 2008).
- Hornung, Alfred. "Terrorist Violence and Transnational Memory: Jonathan Safran Foer and Don DeLillo," *Transnational American Memories*, ed. Udo J. Hebel (Berlin and New York: Walter de Gruyter, 2009), pp. 171–83.
- Kaltenbach, Elisabeth. *Lektürehilfen: Don DeLillo, Falling Man*. Stuttgart: Klett Lerntraining, 2011 (2009).
- Kauffman, Linda S. "The Wake of Terror: Don DeLillo's 'In the Ruins of the Future,' 'Baader-Meinhof,' and *Falling Man*," *Modern Fiction Studies*, 54, no 2 (2008), 353–77.
- Kroes, Rob. "Indecent Exposure: Picturing the Horror of 9/11," *American Multiculturalism after 9/11: Transatlantic Perspectives*, eds Derek Rubin and Jaap Verheul (Amsterdam: Amsterdam University Press, 2009), pp. 67–79.
- Melnick, Jeffrey. *9/11 Culture: America under Construction*. Malden, Massachusetts: Wiley-Blackwell, 2009.
- Olster, Stacey, ed., *Don DeLillo: Mao II, Underworld, Falling Man* (London and New York: Continuum, 2011).
- Poppe, Sandra, Thorsten Schüller, and Sascha Seiler, eds, *9/11 als kulturelle Zäsur: Repräsentationen des 11. September 2001 in kulturellen Diskursen, Literatur und visuellen Medien* (Bielefeld: transcript, 2009).
- Schneck, Peter and Philipp Schweighauser, eds, *Terrorism, Media, and the Ethics of Fiction: Transatlantic Perspectives on Don DeLillo* (New York and London: Continuum, 2010).


## 3. Andere englischsprachige Erzähltexte, die sich mit 9/11 und den Folgen der Terroranschläge beschäftigen


- Amis, Martin. *The Second Plane, September 11: 2001–2007*. London: Vintage, 2008.
- Foer, Jonathan Safran. *Extremely Loud & Incredibly Close*. London: Penguin, 2005.
- Updike, John. "Varieties of Religious Experience," *My Father's Tears and Other Stories* (London: Penguin, 2009), pp. 82–112.


### Bildnachweis